KIDEX for
Ones

Practicing Competent
Child Care for One-Year-Olds

R. Adrienne Boyd, R.N., B.S.N.

THOMSON

DELMAR LEARNING

Australia Canada Mexico Singapore Spain United Kingdom United States

THOMSON

DELMAR LEARNING

KIDEX for Ones: Practicing Competent Child Care for One-Year-Olds
R. Adrienne Boyd, R.N., B.S.N.

Vice President, Career Education SBU:
Dawn Gerrain

Director of Editorial:
Sherry Gomoll

Senior Acquisitions Editor:
Erin O'Connor

Associate Editor:
Chris Shortt

Developmental Editor:
Patricia Osborn

Director of Production:
Wendy A. Troeger

Production Manager:
J.P. Henkel

Production Editor:
Amber Leith

Technology Project Manager:
Sandy Charette

Editorial Assistant:
Stephanie Kelly

Director of Marketing:
Wendy E. Mapstone

Channel Manager:
Kristin McNary

Cover Design:
Joeseph Villanova

Composition:
Pre-Press Company, Inc.

For permission to use material from this text or product, submit a request online at http://www.thomsonrights.com

Any additional questions about permissions can be submitted by email to thomsonrights@thomson.com

Library of Congress Cataloging-in-Publication Data

Boyd, R. Adrienne.
Kidex for ones : practicing competent child care for one-year-olds / R. Adrienne Boyd. p. cm.
Includes bibliographical references and index.
ISBN-10 1-4180-1271-8 (alk. paper)
ISBN-13 978-1-4180-1271-7
1. Day care centers—Administration. 2. Toddlers—Care. I. Title.
HQ778.5.B69 2006
362.71'2—dc22

2005023607

NOTICE TO THE READER

Publisher does not warrant or guarantee any of the products described herein or perform any independent analysis in connection with any of the product information contained herein. Publisher does not assume, and expressly disclaims, any obligation to obtain and include information other than that provided to it by the manufacturer.

The reader is expressly warned to consider and adopt all safety precautions that might be indicated by the activities herein and to avoid all potential hazards. By following the instructions contained herein, the reader willingly assumes all risks in connection with such instructions.

The Publisher makes no representation or warranties of any kind, including but not limited to, the warranties of fitness for particular purpose or merchantability, nor are any such representations implied with respect to the material set forth herein, and the publisher takes no responsibility with respect to such material. The publisher shall not be liable for any special, consequential, or exemplary damages resulting, in whole or part, from the readers' use of, or reliance upon, this material.

The authors and Thomson Delmar Learning affirm that the Web site URLs referenced herein were accurate at the time of printing. However, due to the fluid nature of the Internet, we cannot guarantee their accuracy for the life of the edition.

Contents

Preface

INTRODUCTION

KIDEX for Ones is a proven management tool and essential resource for all child care personnel. It is one of a five-part series that includes KIDEX for one-year-olds, infants, two-year-olds, three-year-olds, and four-year-olds. To assist in providing for competent care for toddlers, *KIDEX for Ones* provides helpful information for start-up and existing programs. To accommodate all the demands of creating a well-planned environment while ensuring children are receiving the best possible care, time-saving suggestions are extremely important. This book provides easy, accessible tools to help you arrange, plan, and organize your program. It offers a format with examples, detailed information, and suggestions to assist you in providing competent child care. *KIDEX for Ones* provides tools that assist communication between staff members. In addition, *KIDEX for Ones* provides forms and templates for keeping active files for each child and suggests a filing system for important information. Essentially, *KIDEX for Ones* will help you, the child care professional, fulfill your role in the daily care of the toddlers you are charged with.

HOW TO USE THIS BOOK

There are eight chapters, three perforated appendices, and a CD-ROM in the back of the book. Many chapters include examples of appropriate forms and/or templates necessary for rendering infant care. The Forms and Templates appendix offers blank duplicates of the examples for you to photocopy, and the CD-ROM enables you to customize the forms according to your specific state standards and center requirements. The chapter examples (also indicated as figures) are there to guide you in completing your own forms when you are ready to use them.

KIDEX for Ones begins with suggestions for how to create a suitable environment equipped to render care and moves on to provide guidance and class management tools helpful for accomplishing physical care of the children. Where readers begin will depend on the degree of guidance they are seeking. For instance, someone in a brand new program would best start at the beginning and work through to the end. Someone in an already existing program searching to strengthen only certain aspects might choose to skip around the various chapters.

- Chapter 1, "Toddlers and One-Year-Old Behavior," profiles patterns and characteristics of toddler behavior and offers suggestions for establishing daily activities. Also covered are suitable expectations of toddlers for the ages of 13–15 months, 16–18 months, 19–21 months, and 22–24 months.

- Chapter 2, "Creating and Organizing a Toddler Room," provides guidance for creating environments that take into account toddlers' specific needs, best arranging the room to accommodate a toddler group's natural tendencies, and accommodating their visiting family members.

- Chapter 3, "Establishing an Excellent Path for Communication," provides classroom management tools to maximize communication between the children's families and all personnel that are involved with your program on a daily basis. It also provides the tools for developing written plans beginning with detailed examples and instructions for assembling a KIDEX Class Book. A KIDEX Class Book is similar to an operating manual for your individual group. Use the examples and templates to write an organized plan for the one-year-old group, including detailed daily schedules, individual profiles pertinent to toddlers' specific needs, lesson plans, and so forth.

- Chapter 4, "Hygiene, Cleaning, and Disinfecting," will help you establish hygienic practices such as procedures for diapering, hand washing, and sanitation.

- Chapter 5, "Health," provides guidance with regard to medications, measuring body temperatures, recording individual illnesses, establishing practices to track illness trends, and other health tips.

- Chapter 6, "Safety," addresses accident and incident reporting, establishing practices to track accident or incident trends, and how to conduct emergency evacuation drills. This chapter also provides tools for recording drills, first aid instructions, and other general safety practices.

- Chapter 7, "Facilitating Toddlers and Their Families," provides suggestions that are conducive for rendering daily toddler care and measures to include the family. The chapter suggests ways to assist both the child and the family from the moment the child is received in the center to daily departure. Some examples of forms include infant receiving sheets, the Introduce Us to Your Toddler form, and individual child profiles for teachers to keep a written record of each individual toddler's activities and progress.

- Chapter 8, "Educational Articles for Families and Staff," provides short articles relevant to the care and understanding of one-year-olds. Use these articles to post on the Current Events Bulletin Board, to print in program newsletters, or as a basis for a parenting and staff education classes. Store copies of these articles and other information you collect for the KIDEX Class Book for future reference.

FEATURES

- Over 40 forms are available to assist child care professionals' care for toddlers, including: nutrition schedules, observation sheets, diaper changing procedures, and daily medication sheets.

- An icon appears throughout the book highlighting best practices.

- Best practices identified in the book are in alignment with CDA credential requirements.

BACK OF THE BOOK CD-ROM

■ Customizable forms are available on the back of the book CD-ROM.
Also available on CD:

■ state contact information to search for specific state rules and regulations

■ organizations listed with contact information for further research

■ additional resources for teachers and families

EACH STATE IS DIFFERENT

A directory listing of all state licensing agencies is available online on the National Resource Center for Child Care Health & Safety Web site at http://nrs.uchsc.edu. A reminder appears at the beginning of each chapter in the form of this icon:

To find your specific State's Licensing, Rules and Regulations go to:

http://nrc.uchsc.edu

It is extremely important to research the laws relevant to your own state licensing standards for compliance as well as to your specific child care center and/or facility.

Although you must follow state rules and regulations, most states require minimum standards. It is debatable whether state requirements reflect the highest level of care, also known as best practices. The term *best practices* comes from 981 standards identified by a panel of experts in the early 1990s. These standards were extracted from a compilation titled *Caring for Our Children* provided by three organizations: the American Academy of Pediatrics (AAP), the American Public Health Association (APHA), and the National Resource Center for Health and Safety. Best practices standards were identified as having the greatest impact on reducing frequent or severe disease, disability, and death (morbidity and mortality) in early education and child care settings. *KIDEX for Ones* incorporates these standards, and an icon highlighting best practices appears in the margins to help you identify what is considered best practices.

KIDEX AND THE CDA CREDENTIAL

KIDEX for Ones incorporates essential information that aligns with many of the CDA competencies. There is a growing trend to raise the bar for child care practices in the United States. Many professional organizations manage accreditation systems for early care and teaching programs, such as the National Association of Educating Young Children (NAEYC), National Association of Child Care Professionals (NACCP), and National Association of Childcare (NAC). Accreditation is a voluntary process designed to improve the quality of child care programs by establishing benchmarks for quality. Caregivers who desire to be recognized for demonstrating competence in the early care and education field can pursue a Child Development Associate (CDA) credential. Candidates for the CDA credential are assessed based upon the CDA Competency Standards. The guidelines for the national CDA credential through the Council for Early Childhood Recognition can be found at http://www.cdacouncil.org.

ABOUT THE AUTHOR

Adrienne Boyd, R.N., B.S.N., has dedicated the majority of her professional life to the early care and education field. With over 22 years' experience in the field, Adrienne previously was executive director and co-owner of Somersett Heights Center for Child Care in Indianapolis. During that time she was active in the community, serving on the Governor's Task Force for Juvenile Justice, Indiana Task Force for Step Ahead Program, the advisory board for the local high school child care vocational school, and the Child Development Training Committee Workgroup on Early Care.

Adrienne served on the National Association of Child Care Professionals (NACCP) board, as a validator for the National Accreditation Commission for Early Child Care and Education Programs (NAC), and continues to serve the Editorial Advisory Board for *Early Childhood News,* a national publication for child care professionals.

In 1995, Adrienne and her husband, Bob, launched Child Development Services, Inc. Through this venue they published manuals, books, and child care training videos. She has received many Directors' Choice Awards for her work. She has contributed and published several articles for *Early Childhood News and Professional Connections,* the trade publication for the National Association of Child Care Professionals.

She is a mother of two grown sons, John and Alexander, and resides with her husband in Lebanon, Indiana.

ACKNOWLEDGMENTS

Throughout the process of writing this material, there were many individuals who supported, encouraged, and shared their expertise. I wish to extend my deepest gratitude to all of you.

To my husband, Bob, and two sons, John and Alexander, for accompanying me on my journey as owner and director of Somersett Heights Center for Child Care.

To Annette Wilson, who so patiently transcribed my writing. To Patricia Osborn, who provided editorial assistance during the revisions of this text. And to the Thomson Delmar Learning staff who caught my vision and helped to give birth to this project. To my sister Lois who so eloquently captures the imagination of children I have had the privilege of working with throughout my early care and education profession.

To my sister Nancy for her great love of children and for how it is a source of inspiration to me. And, finally, love and appreciation to my mother, Helen Struck, my very first teacher.

REVIEWERS

I would like to thank and acknowledge the following highly respected professionals in the child care field who provided invaluable suggestions, comments, and feedback on *KIDEX for Ones* to help make it the effective tool it is.

Patricia Capistron
Lead Teacher
Rocking Unicorn Pre-School
West Chatham, MA

Cheryl Cranston, M.Ed.
Assistant Director of Early
   Education for the Northwest
   Region of ACSI
Gresham, OR

Vicki Folds, Ed.D.
Director of Curriculum
    Development
Children of America
Parkland, FL

Patricia Forkan, M.S.
Executive Director
TLC Learning Center
Blue Island, IL

Marsha Hutchinson, M.Ed., M. Divinity
Executive Director
Polly Panda Preschool
Indianapolis, IN

Nan Howkins
Administrator, Child Care
    Consultant
The Children's Corner
Ridgefield, CT

Bonnie Malakie
Head Start Director Orleans
    Community Action Committee
Albion, NY

Jody Martin
Education and Training Coordinator
Crème de la Crème
Aurora, CO

Wendy McEarchern, M.A.,
    Early Childhood Ed.
Executive Director
Gulf Regional Childcare
    Management Agency
Mobile, AL

Linda Rivers, M.S.
Instructor
Director of Child Care Center
    and Learning Lab
University of Tennessee
Chattanooga, TN

To find your specific
State's Licensing, Rules
and Regulations go to:

http://nrc.uchsc.edu

Toddlers and One-Year-Old Behavior

CHAPTER

1

A comprehensive understanding of toddler nature and behavior provides the foundation for a well-run program. By the time toddlers reach their first birthday they are quickly emerging from babyhood. Their biggest task this year is to establish themselves as independent human beings. The artist Michelangelo once spoke of one of his famous sculptures; when asked how he created it, he answered, "I saw the angel in the marble and carved until I set him free." That is not dissimilar to the work of toddlers as they uncover their emerging selves.

Just as we would not consider forcing toddlers to grow an inch taller, we should not push them to accomplish more than they are capable of before they are ready. Thus, a broad understanding of normal development will help tremendously in the care of toddlers. Understanding their natural patterns of growth and development will help you discern what to ignore as a passing phase and what is important to pay closer attention to.

Toddlers are naturally very self-centered. This focus is necessary for them to develop as individuals. They are in constant motion and are learning the rudimentary skills of decision making, self-sufficiency, self-discipline, and how to assert their influence with others and the environment they inhabit. They are charged with these tasks lacking knowledge of acceptable social skills, possessing minimal vocabulary, and inhabiting a body that has yet to master mobility, coupled with a driving internal force to go forth! Because of their limited repertoire of skills and at times an intense inner drive to break out of their shell, they are bound to experience moments of great frustration.

The period directly following a toddler's first birthday can usually be considered calm. They are delighted with their newest skills and are usually in a pleasant frame of mind. They are still very amenable and easily redirected by methods of distraction. At this age most toddlers have achieved some level of mobility in the form of crawling, pulling up and cruising around the furniture, or walking with or without assistance. They are beginning to grasp objects and babble a few words such as *mama* and *dada*. They usually enjoy lap games and are beginning to recognize and identify their own body parts. In the next few months most toddlers will walk independently, drink from a cup, enjoy looking at books, and scribble on paper with a fat crayon. They will use a spoon intermittently, although it will be some time before they have mastered the use of eating utensils.

As toddlers move into the period between 16 and 18 months, they are continuing to build their skills and are moving toward more assertive behavior. Dr. Louise Bates Ames, with the renowned Gesell Institute, indicates that her "observation of the development of emotional behavior in the growing infant and child has revealed that from earliest infancy on, ages of emotional equilibrium tend to alternate with ages of disequilibrium" (p. 15). Based on the institute's research, one can expect the first half of each age to be a calmer and smoother experience and as the child moves closer to the second half of each year he or she will experience more turbulence and disturbances in behavior. Armed with that information, we can expect toddlers to begin to test limits in many areas as they approach their second birthday. Defiant behavior and the use of the word *no* will begin to surface as they test their new independence. When life becomes too overwhelming toddlers will experience "mini meltdowns" most adults refer to as temper tantrums.

Although their vocabulary continues to grow and they are beginning to combine some words, children of this age still are not capable of clearly expressing many of their needs and desires. Add to this impulsive behavior and less-refined motor skills, and they experience many moments of frustration. Imagine for a moment how challenging it would be to travel in a foreign country and not possess the ability to speak the local language. Depending on your physical energy level, state of mind, and level of hunger, making the simplest requests would at some point become an exhausting endeavor. The situation would certainly generate great moments of frustration until your skills improved, which is not likely to occur quickly. For this same reason it is beneficial to continually help toddlers identify what they are experiencing or feeling. Slowly, over a considerable period of time, they begin to associate your words with their experience. Teaching and using sign language symbols with babies and toddlers is a rapidly growing trend in this country. Research has proven that children who learn basic sign language symbols are less frustrated and their use of verbal language accelerates at a quicker pace. Recommended resources for this practice are located in Chapter 7, "Facilitating Toddlers and Their Families."

Children love to play with balls and musical instruments at this age or bang a spoon loudly on pots and pans. By now books have become a very important tool for discovery and they are able to turn two or three pages at one time. Continue to choose sturdy books made of cloth, vinyl, or heavy cardboard. Paper books require close supervision. Ripping pages is a delightful experiment, and torn paper can be a source of choking. Toddlers are interested in removing clothing by now and might go through a phase of stripping! They are beginning to understand more words than they can say and can follow simple instructions. As the defiant behavior begins to intensify, try not to be disappointed if they don't readily comply with your desires. They are exploring their newfound independence. They will need plenty of practice during this age testing the difference between complying with your needs and asserting their own wants. For later success in life, it is crucial for them to master this ability. An English rock band, The Beatles, once published a song called "Hello, Goodbye" with the words "you say yes, I say no, you say why, I say I don't know . . . you say goodbye and I say hello," which clearly describes similar contradictions toddlers confront each day as they move through this intense phase of their existence. Patience and acceptance from you will help them achieve their goals and lay the groundwork for strong self-esteem. Hang on, for this too will pass.

The time leading up to 21 months will bring on an avalanche of ability. They are chattering new words, though often mispronounced, and are using a couple of dozen words regularly. They know their own names and those of their family and peers. At this point toddlers love to mimic behavior, and matching games are fun. They thoroughly enjoy songs, nursery rhymes, finger plays, play dough, paints, and crayons.

At this juncture it is probably a good time to discuss their play habits and ability to share with their peers. It is fair to say they are operating on a short fuse during most of this period. Their growth and development demand so much of their self-focus they have little ability to practice the best social skills. Sharing is not a top priority! If they want something, they take it. If someone is in their path, they might step on him or her. Biting and hair pulling often are the quickest way to communicate "me first." It is important to encourage them to begin using methods of self-control and self-discipline, but keep in mind most of them are not up for the task consistently.

Buy two or three duplicates of favorite toys for the group, use redirection through distraction, physically move their bodies from temptation or potential harm, remove the object of concern, and create areas for children to play undisturbed until they are able to practice more restraint.

As toddlers move closer to their second birthday most will have grown to three times their birth size. Their skills have grown exponentially since the beginning of the year. They begin to exhibit calming behavior. Most are able to jump up, negotiate stairs, walk, and run. They enjoy puzzles with one to three pieces, stringing large beads, building blocks, circle games, and short stories. They are able to sing some songs, can carry on a conversation with two or three sentences, and are able to speak and be understood a great deal of the time. Some favorite activities involve sensory experiences such as water play, sand play, and exploring outdoors. If you don't provide sand play indoors, consider using dry oatmeal or corn meal as a substitute in the water/sand table.

Children are more capable now at distinguishing between what is yours and what is mine and exercise some degree of self-control in those matters. Some precocious toddlers might begin potty training, although most will be more interested in this pursuit after they are two or two and a half.

Working with toddlers is very demanding work. It requires a great deal of understanding and patience. Yet, it's hard to imagine a more joyful moment than watching a toddler learn to take that first step. And as challenging as a temper tantrum or display of defiance can be, it is comforting to know that behavior is as normal as rain from the sky. In short, if you have the opportunity to share the roller coaster ride one year of age brings, the rewards of watching what children accomplish each step of the way will far outweigh the challenges in a given day.

REFERENCES

Ames, L. B., Ilg, F. L., & Haber, C. C. (1982). *Your one-year-old.* New York: Dell.

McCartney, P. (1967). Hello, Goodbye. In *Hello, Goodbye.* United Kingdom: Capitol.

Michelangelo, quote. Retrieved from http://quotations.about.com/od/stillmorefamouspeople/a/Michelangelo1.htm

RECOMMENDED RESOURCES

Ames, L. B., & Ilg, F. L. (1982). *Your one-year-old.* New York: Dell.

Ellison, S., & Ferdinandi, S. (1996). *365 days of baby love.* Naperville, IL: Sourcebook.

Fisher, J. (1988). *From baby to toddler.* New York: The Berkley Publishing Group.

Healy, J. M. (1987, 1994). *Your child's growing mind.* New York: Dell.

McCourt, L. (2000). *101 ways to raise a happy toddler.* Lincolnwood, IL: Lowell House.

SUPPLY AND EQUIPMENT RESOURCES

ECMD Early Childhood Manufacturer's Direct Supply/Equipment Catalog, 1-800-896-9951, http://www.ecmdstore.com

Educational Resources Catalog, 1-877-877-2805, http://www.edresources.com

CHAPTER

2

To find your specific
State's Licensing, Rules
and Regulations go to:

http://nrc.uchsc.edu

Creating and Organizing a Toddler Room

The quality of a child's environment can have a significant impact on his or her emotional well-being. Healthy children require a safe physical environment in which to eat, sleep, and play in order to accommodate their growth and developmental needs. A well-thought-out room, properly equipped, clean, organized, and well-maintained environment will support their growing needs (see Figure 2–1).

SQUARE FOOTAGE CONSIDERATIONS

There is always a fine balance between meeting local government mandates and considering the cost of your finished space. The minimum standards for licensure differ from state to state. Check your local governing body to determine the guidelines for programs in your area. Plan on at least 35 square feet of indoor space per child. Having more square footage available increases opportunities to create more optimum play spaces. On the other hand, a room that is oversized might prove challenging for toddlers and their teachers since the

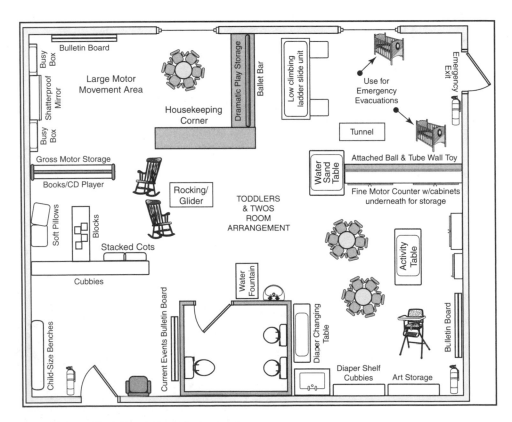

FIGURE 2–1 Toddlers' Rooms Layout

little ones have not established the ability to exercise self-control with boundaries yet. Opt for as much space as is financially feasible when planning your toddler room. Then plan to arrange the room in a manner that discourages running and sprinting about. Square footage costs vary among regions and will be an important factor to consider when determining the most financially feasible size for a facility.

SUGGESTED ROOM LAYOUTS AND ARRANGEMENTS

When planning space to care for toddlers there are some specific ideas to bear in mind. Since it is in the nature of the one-year-old to be very active, mobile, and impulsive, it is imperative that you arrange the room in a manner that encourages their natural inclinations yet serves the needs of the whole group. Plan to create areas that form natural boundaries by constructing knee walls (walls with a ledge about 24" high) or shelves for toys that are too tall to climb on but low enough to avoid obstructing the teachers' view. It's important to secure all lateral pieces of equipment, such as cubbies and toy shelves, securely to the floor or wall to prevent their tipping in the event a toddler attempts an unplanned climbing expedition.

Toddlers need activities they can enjoy throughout the day that do not require teacher interaction. Such activities might include a low-level stair climber or soft climbing center. Many toddler-size activity centers provide opportunities for climbing, sliding, crawling, and going through tunnels. Hang a ballet bar for them to practice pulling up and cruising. Securely fasten a large tube to the wall (made from PVC piping found in the plumbing section of a hardware store) and provide a basket of tennis balls to drop in one end and catch in a basket at the other. Choose a pipe that is larger than their arm circumference and smaller than their head circumference to avoid body parts getting stuck! Other interesting discovery centers to mount on the wall are shatterproof mirrors, busy boxes, and Plexiglas display centers for displaying an assortment of pictures. Hang all pieces of equipment at children's eye level or within a comfortable reach. If the budget permits, a fish aquarium is a delightful center for observation. Pet stores often lease fish aquariums and will provide the food and regular maintenance all in the cost of the lease.

ESTABLISHING PLAY CENTERS

Devote a large amount of space to the active play area where gross motor activities occur. Small feet-driven riding toys, push and pull toys, large dump trucks, and so on need plenty of space. Since toddlers don't have a good sense of boundaries, it is not advisable to locate creative activities such as building blocks near movement activities; otherwise, they will constantly experience crashes. Once children are a year older, the block corner will fit nicely in the active play center. Instructions for making giant building blocks appear in Figure 2–2. The housekeeping, dramatic play, and toy centers work well together. To conserve space,

---

LARGE HOMEMADE BLOCKS

Remove the tops of four ½ gallon paper milk cartons. (Substitute shoe boxes or tissue boxes if necessary.) Stuff one with wadded newspaper. Slide the remaining container over the stuffed container. Cover the block with brightly colored contact paper to extend its durability. The toddlers will have great fun stacking these blocks!

FIGURE 2–2 Homemade Blocks

consider placing eating, art, and fine motor activity centers close to each other. Place these areas near a source of running water to assist with water and sand activities, art exploration, snack and meal times, and cleanup.

Create a quiet area for peaceful exploration or daydreaming without interruption. A space that provides natural boundaries such as soft cushions and pillows will provide a place for toddlers to decompress or be by themselves for a short while before rejoining the group. A library center is another place for the toddler to experience solitary play. Locate it away from active play, and stock it with sturdy books and soft seating or mats. Because some child care providers use playpens as a quiet area to establish boundaries for children, it is important to address the most current trend of thinking among "best practice" professionals. First of all, most state licensing regulators prohibit using playpens or cribs for any reason other than sleeping or diaper changing. Using equipment that restrains a child's physical movements, such as swings, walkers, playpens, and cribs, as areas for playing is strongly discouraged. Restricting toddlers' ability to move slows down their development and their ability to explore their body without restraint. Subjecting toddlers to long periods in restrictive equipment reduces their stimulating experiences and hinders healthy growth and development.

Plan your play spaces so they are accessible to children with special needs. Although some children with special needs will need help adapting toys for their use, most will not require specially designed toys. *Children with Special Needs in Early Childhood Settings* (Paasche, Gorrill, & Strom 2004) is a wonderful resource book to assist with identifying, intervening with, and including special needs children in your early care and education program.

Clean-up time will be made easier by labeling all the toys, equipment, bookshelves, and clothing hooks with pictures that match where items are to be returned. Cover the pictures with clear contact paper to protect them. Of course, toddlers are just beginning to learn how to match toys and other items with pictures. They will require a great deal of assistance, but it is a necessary part of their growth. Some days they will cooperate better than others. Treating clean-up time as a fun activity often helps. For instance, have them gather "mail" (blocks) to put in the "mailbox" (the block container you are holding) while you act as if you are the postmaster!

OUTDOOR PLAY SPACES

Give toddlers daily opportunities year round to play outdoors. It is important to provide a space for toddlers to play separate from older children. Many state licensing agencies require separated playgrounds for infants and toddlers. Toddlers' play habits are completely different and they are more likely to sustain an injury if they are grouped with older children. Provide the toddlers play equipment and materials suitable for their level of development. Playgrounds today need to offer children opportunities to use their bodies and imagination. Vogel (1997) suggests "in the outdoor area children enjoy swinging, running, climbing, balancing, digging, pedaling, throwing, and catching" (p. 35). Create a soft fall zone under and around all climbing and play equipment. An area with a hard surface will provide opportunities for riding toys. Children should wear proper safety helmets when using riding toys to protect then from dangerous head injuries. A great deal of planning is necessary to design and construct a modern playground that is equipped with safe materials and play equipment that is also accessible to children with special needs. The play equipment and surfaces need to conform to recommendations from the American with Disabilities Act (ADA). For guidance to build, equip, and inspect a playground that meets all suggested standards of accessibility and safety requirements, refer to the recommended resources at the end of this chapter.

MUSIC AND LIGHTING

Sunlight, bright lighting, peaceful music and sounds provide a sense of well-being and can encourage pleasant and cheerful feelings among those who occupy the space. It is a well-documented fact that children require low-stress environments to thrive. Provide several sources of music and lighting to enhance the toddler room and promote a peaceful, home-like atmosphere. Soft lighting is soothing for resting and napping children. Wire the rooms to create soft lighting in the resting and quiet areas. Table lamps are another alternative if wiring a more sophisticated lighting pattern is not feasible. Skylights also provide a gentle, natural lighting source. Check with your local licensing agents to determine the amount of lighting mandated during waking and sleeping times, since requirements vary from state to state.

Activities such as singing, playing, and listening to music support positive change in the brain and increase intelligence. Current research tells us that reading and singing to children are a simple and effective way to promote brain development. Music serves many functions in the early care and teaching environment. An *ABC Primetime* producer (Harrington 1994) reported that "scientific research has linked the use of music with increasing brain development. A PET Scan (positron emission tomography) scans and measures brain activities with actual pictures that demonstrate once stimulation is applied repetitively, in a positive fashion, actual connections in the brain sprout and grow new brain pathways." Studies have demonstrated that Mozart, Classical, and Baroque music, strengthens the pathways in the brain for future math development! Children enjoy many different musical experiences. Feel free to experiment with a wide variety of music from classical lullabies to the exciting sounds of marching and parade music. A vast amount of literature describes how the brain develops in the early years and suggests measures to facilitate growth. The National Child Care Information Centers (NCCIC) is a national clearinghouse and technical assistance center. Its mission is to link parents, care providers, policy makers, researchers, and the public to early care and education information http://www.nccic.org.

BATHROOM AND DIAPERING AREA

Most toddlers don't embark on a serious toilet training program until they are two or older. There is a wide disparity between being able to control the muscles needed to perform the task and possessing the emotional maturity and desire to achieve independent toilet use. Be prepared, though, for when a toddler does express a desire to begin.

Equip the bathrooms with flushing toilets. Special child-size flushing toilets are available so children can sit on the toilet and touch the floor with their feet. There are many available alternatives for adapting larger toilets for toddler use. Many toddlers seem comfortable with portable potty chairs because they are small and do not have a "frightening" flush. It is important to check with your licensing agency for specific guidelines on equipping toddlers' bathrooms. The rules tend to vary from state to state. Even if most children are not yet toilet trained, the flushing toilets will provide a handy and safe area to discard soiled soap, water, and disinfecting solutions created by daily cleansing of soiled diapers and soiled clothing containers.

Most early care and education environments opt to use disposable diapers, training pants, bibs, or wipes in place of cloth in order to promote the highest level of sanitary practice. However, sometimes children are allergic to the materials found in disposable diapers and require the use of cloth diapers. If cloth diapers are used for children with medical conditions such as allergies, special handling during changing will be necessary to ensure hygiene and safety for the handlers. Diaper changing procedures are explored in greater detail in Chapter 4, "Hygiene, Cleaning, and Disinfecting."

The diapering area will require a nonabsorbent changing surface, running water at an adult height, liquid soap with a pump or dispenser, disposable nonabsorbent gloves, nonabsorbent paper liners, disposable wipes, each child's personally labeled physician-prescribed ointments, diapers, cotton balls, plastic bags, tissues, a lidded hands-free plastic-lined trash container, disinfectant, and paper towels. If cloth diapers are used, prepare a special receptacle to collect the soiled cloth diapers. Prepare a washable container labeled "soiled cloth diapers" and a tightly lidded, hands-free, plastic-lined receptacle. Soiled cloth diapers don't require separate bagging. However, any soiled diapers sent home are to be secured in a plastic bag, separate from soiled clothing. Clean and disinfect the receptacle daily, and dispose of waste water in a toilet or floor drain only.

Several varieties of diaper changing tables are available on the market today. Some of the tables are equipped with pull-out staircases. The children can walk up the steps, with assistance, to the changing mat. Considering the number of diapers changed on a given day in a toddler room, the steps help reduce injuries a teacher might experience over time from frequent lifting. It is also useful for teachers to wear safety support belts when performing tasks repeatedly. They provide extra support for the back.

If you don't choose a diaper table that provides space for individual storage for each child's personal supplies, then mount shelves above the changing area to store each individual child's supplies.

Instruct a plumber to install two sinks, one at an adult's height and one at a child's height, next to the changing table, as well as a water fountain at a child's height. All sources of hot water feeding into the room will require an antiscald device. Devise a turn-off valve for available water sources, out of reach of little hands but convenient to yours, to avoid unnecessary water exploration.

SLEEPING AND NAPPING AREA

By the time toddlers reach one year of age, they can quickly adapt to cots for their rest and napping periods. Cots are available in several varieties. Choose cots that can withstand regular sanitizing and will store easily, in a compact manner, to save space. It is still a good idea to have one or two cribs in the room. A crib serves multiple uses in a toddler setting. The crib can provide a familiar area for a toddler who is just transitioning from an infant room or who is new to group care. They often find a crib more comforting while they become familiar with the new routine. If the center does not have dedicated space for a sick bay area, the cribs can serve as a temporary isolation area in the event one of the toddlers becomes ill. The toddler can rest with the least amount of disturbance in a crib until his or her parents are able to call for him or her. The cribs can also be used to push the children to a designated area during a safety evacuation. Evacuation procedures are discussed in Chapter 6, "Safety." Equip the cribs with sturdy casters. Casters are available in most supply catalogs listed at the end of this chapter.

Some toddlers enjoy rocking and cuddling prior to napping. Place several gliding rocking chairs in your toddler rooms. A gliding chair provides a rocking motion without the hazard of pinching a crawling toddler's fingers. Glider rocking chairs are available in baby superstores and can be found at Early Childhood Manufacturers' Direct at http://www.ECMDStore.com or 1-800-896-9951. Create a quiet play area equipped with books, puzzles, and table activities where the first few awakening toddlers can enjoy the last few moments of nap time before all of the children have awakened.

STORING PERSONAL BELONGINGS/CUBBIES

Avoid spreading germs and the potential cross-contamination of each child's personal articles. Personal belongings such as coats, hats, and extra clothing are best kept in separate cubbies. Consider creating a space near the entrance door or in an area that will handle heavy traffic in the busy arrival and departure hours. Commercial cubby or locker units are widely marketed in school catalogs such as Discount School Supply (http://www.DiscountSchoolSupply.com or 1-800-627-2829) or KAPLAN Early Learning Company (http://www.kaplanco.com or 1-800-334-2014).

SELECTING APPROPRIATE TOYS

Toys are props used in play by all children. Play is valuable for all areas of growth and development. There are some basic facts to consider when choosing toys for children under the age of three. It is their nature to explore just about everything by putting them in their mouths, banging them, or exploring them through their sense of touch. Choose toys that are sturdy and capable of withstanding repeated washing and disinfecting. One-year-olds are fascinated with cause and effect. It is their way of figuring out the world they live in. Push and pull toys, pop-up toys, and toys that react to their touch offer plenty of cause-and-effect practice. Toys that allow them to collect items and dump them are a favorite of toddlers. Suspend a bucket from the ceiling and fill it with blocks or large plastic pop toys; children will enjoy many hours filling and dumping the bucket. Large dump trucks are also a great source of fun. Choose sturdy models in case they decide to explore riding on the trucks themselves! Provide a variety of blocks, both soft and hard, or blocks with textures. Children will use them in a variety of ways, such as building rudimentary towers, lining them up, or using them for filling and dumping activities.

Safety is another important concern. Having too many toys out at once can be overwhelming and cause a tripping hazard. Limit the amount of toys on the floor at a given time. Select toys that do not present a strangulation or choking hazard. Steer clear of small removable parts, knobs, or beads. Avoid stuffed animals or dolls with detachable eyes, such as button eyes. Purchase a "no-choke testing tube," available at some toy stores. If an object fits in the tube, then it is considered potentially dangerous and should not be used by children under age three. Small balls and latex balloons are dangerous and should be avoided. Mylar balloons are a safer choice. Avoid using toys with long cords or strings in order to avoid strangulation. Shorten cords or strings on pull toys or clothing to no longer than 12 inches. Stuffed animals are best individually labeled and used by one child only during their resting period. Avoid items with sharp edges. Toys with sharp edges or broken pieces are a potential danger; remove them immediately. Heed warning labels on toys. They are placed there by law in the United States. The Consumer Product Safety Commission (CPSC) has the authority to recall dangerous toys and products from the market. Also, the mission of state Public Interest Research Groups (PIRGs) is to help educate toy purchasers to avoid the most common hazards in toys. For a complete list of toy tips and safety e-mail alerts, contact http://www.toysafety.com.

Brain development research has provided sound evidence that reading to children for as little as 15–20 minutes per day from an early age contributes to a myriad of positive brain developments. Early care and education professionals are well aware that reading helps develop children's attention span, builds vocabularies, enhances self-esteem, increases the ability to visualize and imagine, and provides many opportunities to understand words and spoken language. Based on this evidence, an enriched environment for toddlers is filled with pictures and books that contain simple stories, rhymes, and finger plays. Select picture and board books. Board books are sturdy books specifically designed for very young children with pages that are easy for children to turn. Board books generally have brightly colored pictures and simple stories, rhyming words, and repetitive phrases that appeal to young children. The following teacher-recommended books are good choices for toddlers:

Hop on Pop by Dr. Seuss

The Very Hungry Caterpillar by Eric Carle

Goodnight Moon by Margaret Wise Brown

Green Eggs and Ham by Dr. Seuss

Jesse Bear, What Will You Wear? by Nancy White Carlstrom

Freight Train by Donald Crews

Who Hops? by Katie Davis

In the Tall, Tall Grass by Denise Fleming

Time for Bed by Mem Fox

My Trucks by Kristen Hall

Who's Mouse Are You? By Robert Kraus

Becca Backward, Becca Frontward by Bruce McMillan

Ted in a Red Bed by Avil Cox

Biscuit by Anissa Capucilli

Don't be surprised if toddlers want you to read the same books repeatedly. One-year-olds often enjoy different variations of how the story ends or your inserting their name in place of a character's name. Once they move closer to age two they often will reach a stage where they insist on the "exact" story. Until then, enjoy exploring the variety of ways a story can be told.

Consider a few final thoughts when choosing toys for children in and out of a home setting. In a group of toddlers, there will always be favorite toys. Toddlers have a very limited capacity to understand sharing. Many potential skirmishes can be avoided if toddlers are not expected to share and several copies of duplicate toys and books are provided. For a selection of suggested toys and equipment, see Figure 2–3.

CHOOSING TOYS WITH CULTURAL DIVERSITY IN MIND

Responsible early care and teaching programs strive to address diversity in the classroom. Special thought and planning are required to create a diverse environment that is considerate of different genders and racial and ethnic differences encountered within our population. In order to integrate appropriate practices, choose toys that include all the backgrounds and cultures represented in the community and your classroom. Make an effort to choose dolls with different colored skins. Display pictures that represent all nationalities. Seek help from the parents to explore other areas such as food, words children are familiar with, music they hear in their own family environment, or special holidays they celebrate. Parents will appreciate your effort to include them in the process of integrating practices that recognize the various cultures their children represent.

EQUIPMENT AND SUPPLIES FOR TODDLERS

EQUIPMENT & TOYS:

bird feeder
busy boxes mounted on wall
felt board
goldfish
hooks mounted on board
hook permanently installed on
    ceiling
large pegs and pegboard
large blanket
mirror (full-size)
nesting blocks
play dishes
pop beads
ramp (3–4 inch wide board)
several dishpans
several sorting cubes
several puppets
variety of push toys
washable variety of stuffed animals
wooden blocks, all sizes

FOOD SUPPLIES:

cold cooked spaghetti
crackers
dry beans
empty ½ gallon jugs with lids, glue
ice cream
gelatin (plain or flavored)
flavored drink powder
large ice cubes
lemon
milk
oatmeal or cornmeal
oranges, cucumbers, potatoes
oyster crackers in paper cups
peanut butter
pickles
plastic pop bottle, oil, food coloring,
    glue lid
pudding for painting
sugar cookies, icing, & decorations

MUSICAL:

blank tapes
CD/tape of different kinds of trans-
    portation sounds
CD/tape of water sounds
CD/tape of weather sounds

jack-in-the-box
lullaby music
musical instruments
noisemaker for shaking
nursery rhyme tapes/CDs
object flash cards
old pots and pans
parade music tapes/CDs
rattles
tape recorder/CD player
variety of bells (designed for infants
    and toddlers only)
xylophone

BOOKS AND PICTURES:

animal pictures
animal pictures for 2-piece puzzles
book of zoo animals
books with real photos of children
    of all cultures
book of pictures of different kinds
    of houses
community people book
everyday items covered with
    contact paper
farm animal book
laminated pictures of farm animals
matching pictures & objects, glued
    in containers
mount leaves & cover with contact
    paper
nursery rhyme book
old magazines/toy catalogues
picture books
picture of sun and moon, laminated
pictures of different kinds of
    transportation
pictures of dogs and cats
pictures of fish
Richard Scarry book *Things That Go*
story of seasons
simple picture books/board books
simple story books
touch and feel books

ART SUPPLIES:

colorful fabric swatches/different
    textures
contact paper

cotton balls
dark construction paper
glue
jumbo crayons
multicultural crayons, paint, &
    paper (full range of skin colors)
masking tape
nontoxic colored markers
nontoxic color chart
nontoxic finger paints
packing peanuts (use
    biodegradable ones made
    from potato starch)
paper towel rolls
paper plates
paper cups
pieces of netting material
sandpaper
sand (gallon container)
shaving cream*
small paint brushes
sponges, different shapes & sizes
straws
toilet paper rolls
tree leaves
wax paper

GENERAL SUPPLIES:

adult rocking chairs
balls, all sizes
beach ball
bristle blocks or Duplo blocks
bubbles
buckets
cardboard boxes
carpet squares
chairs with arms
cloth bag or pillow case
coffee cans & plastic rings
colored scarves
cots
dolls representing a variety of
    cultures and both genders
dress-up clothes
egg cartons
empty match boxes
flash light
large beads for stringing
low slide

Some states do not allow the use of shaving cream. Check your regulations.

FIGURE 2-3 Equipment and Supplies List

EQUIPMENT AND SUPPLIES FOR TODDLERS

plastic blocks
plastic salt & pepper shakers
plastic curlers (small)
play telephone
real flowers
several riding toys without pedals
several matching items (mittens,
    socks, flowers)
several "doll" brushes & combs
several plastic jars with lids
several doll "blankets"
several shoe strings
several old purses

several 2–4 piece puzzles
Several pinecones
shoe box
silhouettes & matching tools
small object tester (choke tube)
small cars
small pans
spoons
soft climbers
stacking rings
stair step climber
string for "pretend animal leash,"
    12" or less

tennis balls
texture squares to feel
toddler-size activity centers
used food boxes
variety of feathers
variety of large sea shells
variety of large smooth & rough
    rocks
variety of hats
variety of washable dolls
wind sock
wooden clothespins with container
zippers

FIGURE 2-3 Equipment and Supplies List *(Continued)*

Carol J. Fuhler, author of *Teaching Reading with Multicultural Books Kids Love*, is an excellent resource. She encourages many approaches for a teacher to integrate multicultural teachings relevant in today's culturally diverse society. "[For children] to make a strong connection with a book, to elicit that all-important affective response, every child should see his or her face reflected in some of the illustrations. His or her culture should be explored realistically within well-crafted stories" (p.*x*). A teacher who continually makes a deliberate effort to integrate and explore differences and likeness among all people will provide an environment that communicates acceptance for all children he or she cares for.

ROOM APPEARANCES

It doesn't take long for a busy toddler room to begin to become cluttered. To keep up the center's appearance and maintain a safe environment, always make an effort to reduce clutter and maintain cleanliness in your environment. Without a consistent effort to maintain order, the room appearance and safety will become compromised. A room strewn with unkempt toys is not only unsightly, but creates potential tripping hazards. Furthermore, a room filled with too many toys strewn about can create an overstimulating environment for an active group of toddlers. Toddlers often will lash out with aggressive behavior such as biting, scratching, or hair pulling if they feel stressed and overwhelmed. To avoid putting children in a position they are not equipped to cope with, limit the amount of toys.

Imagine how you prepare your home for a party before guests arrive. You survey the house and stow all miscellaneous clutter in its proper place. The floors are vacuumed, dust is removed, and fingerprints are washed away, leaving the room sparkling and clean. Fresh flowers are always a nice touch. You are motivated to create a pleasant environment for the guests you are about to receive. Think about the environment you create for the children in your care. Imagine that every day is your grand opening. Look around the room and see where a pile of clutter has begun to form. Are toys scattered about the room creating a potential for tripping or falling? Are old magazines, used sippy cups, or used washcloths strewn around? Toddlers will still often put toys in their mouths. A routine for handling soiled toys and soiled clothing is covered in detail in Chapter 4, "Hygiene, Cleaning, and Disinfecting."

Toddler rooms require continual clearing off, cleaning up, and putting away. Establish regular housekeeping routines and post a cleaning schedule (Figure 2–4) for all to

Cleaning Schedule

For the Week of _February 4th_

Classroom _Blueberries_

#	Daily Cleaning Projects	Mon	Tue	Wed	Thr	Fri	Once-A-Week Projects	Initial	Date
1.	Mop floors	C	C	C	C	C	Scrub brush & mop (corners)	CM	2/4
2.	Clean all sinks (use cleanser)	C	C	C	C	C	Wipe down all bathroom walls	LS	2/5
3.	Wipe down walls (around sinks)	C	C	C	C	C	Scrub step stools	LS	2/6
4.	Clean & disinfect toilets (with brush in & out)	C	C	C	C	C	Use toothbrush on fountain (mouth piece)	CM	2/4
5.	Clean water fountains/wipe with disinfectant	C	C	C	C	C	Clean windows	AH	2/7
6.	Clean inside of windows and seals	C	C	C	C	C	Wipe off door handles	AH	2/8
7.	Clean inside & outside glass on doors	C	C	C	C	C	Organize shelves	CM	2/5
8.	Clean & disinfect changing table & under the pad	C	C	C	C	C	Move furniture and sweep	CM	2/4
9.	Run vacuum (carpet & rugs)	C	C	C	C	C	Wipe underneath tables & legs	LS	2/7
10.	Dispose of trash (replace bag in receptacle)	C	C	C	C	C	Wipe chair backs and legs	AH	2/4
11.	Wipe outside of all cans & lids with disinfectant	C	C	C	C	C	Wipe off cubbies/shelves	LS	2/7
12.	Repeat 10 & 11 for diaper pails	C	C	C	C	C	(preschool & older groups) Wipe/sanitize toys	AH	2/8
13.	Clean & disinfect high chairs/tables/chairs	C	C	C	C	C	**Immediate Project**		
14.	Clean & disinfect baby beds/cots	C	C	C	C	C	Any surface area contaminated with body fluids such as blood, stool, mucus, vomit or urine	CM	2/6
15.	Reduce clutter! (Organize!)	C	C	C	C	C	**Quarterly**		
16.	(infant & toddler groups) Wipe/sanitize toys after each individual use	C	C	C	C	C	Clean carpets		
17.	Change crib sheets as directed	C	C	C	C	C			
18.									

Lead Teacher: _Ms. Marshall_ 　　　　C – Complete　　N/A – Not Applicable

FIGURE 2–4 Classroom Cleaning Schedule

follow. Your efforts to create a pleasant environment will make everyone comfortable and will provide the staff with an enjoyable atmosphere to work in. It truly does make a big difference.

References

Fuhler, C. J. (2000). *Teaching reading with multicultural books kids love.* Golden, CO: Fulcrum.

Paasche, C. L., Gorrill, L., & Strom, B. (2004). *Children with special needs in early childhood settings.* Clifton Park, NY: Thomson Delmar Learning.

Vogel, N. (1997). *Getting started.* Ypsilanti, MI: High/Scope Press.

Recommended Resources

American Society for Testing and Materials (ASTM), http://www.astm.org

Bredekamp, S., & Copple, C. (1997). *Developmentally appropriate practice* (Rev. ed.). Washington, DC: National Association for the Education of Young Children.

Hall, N. S. (1999). *Creative resources for the anti-bias classroom.* Clifton Park, NY: Thomson Delmar Learning.

Harms, T., Cryer, D. & Clifford, R. M. (1990). *Infant/toddler environment rating scale.* New York: Teachers College Press.

Healy, J. M. (1994). *Your child's growing mind* (Rev. ed.). New York: Dell Publishing. (Original work published 1987).

Marhoefer, P. E., & Vadnais, L. A. (1988). *Caring for the developing child.* Clifton Park, NY: Thomson Delmar Learning.

National Program for Playground Safety (NPPS), http://www.playgroundsafety.org

Sobut, M. A., & Bogen, B. N. (1991). *Complete early childhood curriculum resource.* West Nyack, NY: The Center for Applied Research in Education.

Talaris Research Institute. *Advancing knowledge of early brain development.* http://www.talaris.org

VanGorp, L. M. (2001). *1001 best websites for parents.* Westminister, CA: Teacher Created Materials.

State Public Interest Research Groups (PIRGs)
218 D Street SE
Washington, DC 20003
202-546-9707
http://www.pirg.org

The Consumer Product Safety Commission (CPSC)
1-800-638-2772
http://www.cpsc.gov
info@cpsc.gov

More Resources for School Supplies and Equipment

United Art and Education, P.O. Box 9219, Fort Wayne, IN 46899, 1-800-322-3247, http://www.unitednow.com

Constructive Playthings, 13201 Arrington Road, Grandview, MO 64030-2886, 1-800-448-4115, http://www.cptoys.com

Kaplan Early Learning Company, P.O. Box 609, Lewisville, NC 27023-0609, 1-800-334-2014, http://www.kaplanco.com

Establishing an Excellent Path for Communication

Achieving excellent communication between the center staff and the families they serve requires a well-managed atmosphere with an attention to detail.

KIDEX FOR ONES CLASS BOOK

A KIDEX Class Book organizes, supports, and promotes consistent toddler care. It is similar to an operating manual for each individual group. *KIDEX for Ones* provides the examples and templates you will need to assemble your own KIDEX Class Book for your group of toddlers. The templates assist the busy lead teacher and other program personnel to create, update, and maintain current written documentation with ease. They are designed for multiple uses and can be photocopied, allowing for adaptation and branding by each individual program. Use the examples and templates to write an organized plan for the toddler group, detailed daily schedules, individual profiles, lesson plans, and so on. Place the KIDEX Class Book in a visible location so the substitute teacher or program personnel can find it at a moment's notice if you are absent or unavailable. The KIDEX Class Book can also serve as a valuable reference at program meetings.

HOW TO ASSEMBLE A KIDEX CLASS BOOK

Figure 3–1 provides a flowchart for creating the KIDEX Class Book. Purchase a 1–2 inch binder, preferably one that has a clear-view front and enough index tabs to create about 16 or 17 sections in the book. Along with each section on the flowchart are the specific figure numbers that will help you locate examples and blank templates. Organize your KIDEX Class Book into sections as indicated on the flowchart. Feel free to customize the KIDEX Class Book and add categories to it that comply with your organization's regulations and goals. Figure 3–2 provides an example of a cover for the KIDEX Class Book. To customize a cover for your own KIDEX Class Book, use the blank template provided in the Forms and Templates appendix and cheerful stationary or center logo paper.

DAILY TODDLER SCHEDULE OUTLINE

The Daily Toddler Schedule Outline located in Figures 3–3 and 3–4 is a *brief* summary of planned daily activities. Its simple format is designed to provide a quick orientation for a substitute teacher and for parents visiting the center. The information found on the Daily Toddler Schedule Outline will give them a *general idea* of what a typical day in the group looks like. It does not contain the same details that are outlined in the Daily Toddler Schedule Details. The Daily Toddler Schedule Details give a more in-depth look at the day, providing information about where to find things, rationales for what is done, and who

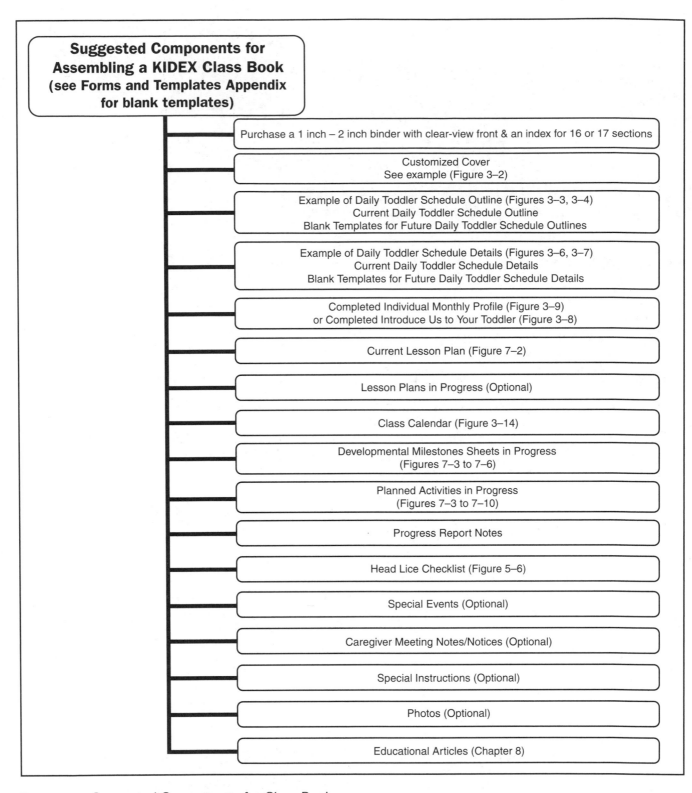

Suggested Components for Assembling a KIDEX Class Book (see Forms and Templates Appendix for blank templates)

Purchase a 1 inch – 2 inch binder with clear-view front & an index for 16 or 17 sections

Customized Cover
See example (Figure 3–2)

Example of Daily Toddler Schedule Outline (Figures 3–3, 3–4)
Current Daily Toddler Schedule Outline
Blank Templates for Future Daily Toddler Schedule Outlines

Example of Daily Toddler Schedule Details (Figures 3–6, 3–7)
Current Daily Toddler Schedule Details
Blank Templates for Future Daily Toddler Schedule Details

Completed Individual Monthly Profile (Figure 3–9)
or Completed Introduce Us to Your Toddler (Figure 3–8)

Current Lesson Plan (Figure 7–2)

Lesson Plans in Progress (Optional)

Class Calendar (Figure 3–14)

Developmental Milestones Sheets in Progress
(Figures 7–3 to 7–6)

Planned Activities in Progress
(Figures 7–3 to 7–10)

Progress Report Notes

Head Lice Checklist (Figure 5–6)

Special Events (Optional)

Caregiver Meeting Notes/Notices (Optional)

Special Instructions (Optional)

Photos (Optional)

Educational Articles (Chapter 8)

FIGURE 3–1 Suggested Components for Class Book

has specific instructions for care. Blank templates for creating your own Daily Toddler Schedule Outline and Daily Toddler Schedule Details are found in the Forms and Templates appendix. Post a copy of the Daily Toddler Schedule Outline on the Current Events Bulletin Board (Figure 3–5) for the parents to view and in your centrally located KIDEX

KIDEX *for* ONES
Class Book

The Blueberries
_____
GROUP NAME

FIGURE 3–2 KIDEX for Ones Class Book—Group Template

DAILY TODDLER SCHEDULE OUTLINE
Nap Schedule-One

Early Morning	Children arrive / hello / health assessment / breakfast / medications as needed / self-directed activities – play centers.
	Morning exercise / music / songs / finger plays / diaper changes if needed
Mid Morning	Diapering / sharing time / clean hands and faces
	Snack time / table time – fine motor activities
	Vocabulary / songs / music (see suggested activities)
	Nap time 1 – 1 1/2 hours / quiet play
Late Morning	Diapering / sharing time / wash hands / clean up nap time cots / outside play
	Wash hands and faces if needed
Mid Day	Lunch time
	Clean up from lunch / medications as needed
	Activity centers – self-directed play
	Art exploration / cognitive choices
Early Afternoon	Afternoon nap time
	(Prepare for afternoon activities / update charting / notes home)
Mid Afternoon	Wake up
	Diaper changes / sharing time / toddler cleanup / hand washing
	Cot cleanup / Snacks
Late Afternoon	Inside play (see suggested activity choices)
	Self-directed activities – play centers
	Final toddler cleanup – comb/brush hair – change soiled clothing
	Diaper changing / hand washing
	Review charts / gather items to send home
Early Evening	Predinner snack, table activities - fine motor
	Departures occurring
	Rocking, music, stories
	Close room and prepare for tomorrow

FIGURE 3–3 Nap Schedule Outline One

DAILY TODDLER SCHEDULE OUTLINE
Nap Schedule-Two

Early Morning	Children arrive, hello, health assessment / breakfast / medications as needed / play centers / self-directed activities / KIDEX activities / morning exercise / music

Mid Morning	Diapering/toileting sharing time / hand washing
	Toddler circle games / Music dance
	Snacks served
	Mini rest
	  songs / finger plays / flannel board / stories / vocabulary
	  art exploration

Late Morning	Outside activities – gross motor play Diaper changes / hand washing / sharing time Look at books and prepare for lunch
Mid Day	Lunch time, medications as needed Clean up lunch Prepare for nap time Nap time begins
Early Afternoon	Diaper changing / sharing time / hand washing Nap time cleanup
Mid Afternoon	Snack time cleanup Outside activities – gross motor play
Late Afternoon	KIDEX activities / Play centers Diaper changes / wash hands and faces / sharing time Change soiled clothing Gather items for departing Stories / puppets / finger plays / vocabulary
Early Evening	Mini snack Table toys / reading / puzzles / blocks Close room and prepare for tomorrow

FIGURE 3–4 Nap Schedule Outline Two

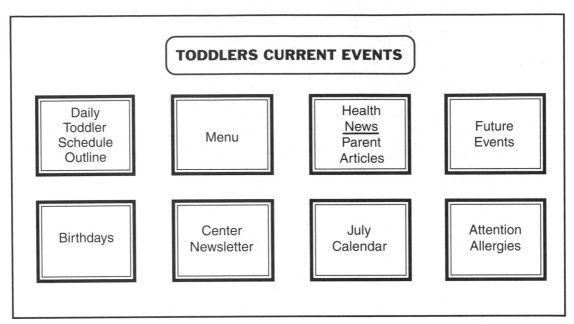

FIGURE 3–5 Current Events Board

Class Book for the substitute teacher to view. It is a good idea to ask a colleague to review your Daily Toddler Schedule Outline and Daily Toddler Schedule Details to verify whether the written instructions reflect your intentions.

Every early care and education provider knows children thrive with a consistent routine. Try to re-create your daily routines in this written form. A successful plan will ensure a consistent day for the toddlers in your absence. Two versions of the schedule outline and the schedule details are available to accommodate one- and two-nap schedules. Refer to Figures 3–3 and 3–4 for examples of the schedule outline and Figures 3–6 and 3–7 for examples of the schedule details. Generally, young toddlers (ages 13–17 months) cope better in a group setting with a two-nap schedule. In a 9–10 hour day, they will tire both mentally and physically, and two naps help keep them feeling their best. Once toddlers are closer to 17 or 18 months, their stamina for coping increases and a one-nap schedule often will suffice.

Notice on the examples for the Daily Toddler Schedule Outline and the Daily Toddler Schedule Details a third predinner snack is suggested. The toddlers in your care in the late afternoon and early evening will sometimes become fussy and irritable because they are hungry or thirsty. It is almost time for their departure, and dinner is often at least an hour away. Toddlers tend to have erratic appetites. Reisser (1997) noted a toddler "may eat voraciously one day and show little interest the next, or consume a sizable breakfast and then quit after only a few bites of the day's other meals" (p. 251). Toddlers are learning how to use eating utensils and may be distracted by other interests when eating, so sometimes they do not consume enough calories to sustain their needs. Planned snacks and meals are necessary to provide adequate nutrition. Endless grazing throughout the day is not advisable. But a few soda crackers, animal crackers, or cheese cubes and some water will help restore their energy. A small program change such as this will result in a quick change from fussy to happy todlers.

DAILY TODDLER SCHEDULE DETAILS
Nap Schedule-One

Early Morning	Ms Lee arrives, opens room, does safety check of environment
	Welcomes each child as they arrive
	Jordan & Erica are usually first to arrive at 6:30, the majority of all children are here by 8:30, Christopher is usually last to arrive at 9:00.
	During this time have several sets of toys out. The busy boxes on the wall and soft slide are favorites.
	Breakfast cart arrives about 6:45 and serving begins
	Danielle is allergic to grapefruit.
	We do a health check, if we notice any problems we contact the family for more details.
	I arrive around 7:45. While Ms. Lee completes the breakfast schedule I give any medications scheduled. I change any diapers needed. Ms. Lee joins me supervising the floor activity cleanup and preparing for our morning exercise (see lesson plan) posted
Mid Morning	Diaper changes begin after early morning activities.
	Ms. Lee continues diaper changes and hand washing and I finish the songs, finger plays and begin to prepare the table and children for snacks.
	Once snacks are finished we clean fingers and hands and table and I proceed with table activities (see lesson plan)
	Ms. Lee prepares cots & blankets.
	We have the toddlers get their "security toys" from their cubbies. This signals to them nap time is about to begin. Bobby and Melissa use a pacifier and they are located in a box in their cubby. It goes back in their cubby after nap. Turn on the nap time music and dim the lights. Jordan likes his back rubbed and falls asleep quickly. Mary falls asleep kicking her shoe rhythmically. Nap time lasts about 1 hour.
	This is a good time to catch up on charting and take turns for a break in the room.
Late Morning	As the children begin to wake up I begin diapering and hand washing procedures as
	Ms. Lee cleans up the cots and blankets and prepares the children for outdoors.
	We play on our toddler playground outside. If it's raining see rainy day box in the closet.
Mid Day	Lunch is delivered about 11:30. While Ms. Lee supervises the hand washing and lunch I set up the self-directed play centers. Only direct 1 or 2 toddlers to each play center and help them begin the activity. Once they begin to engage in the activity move away and help others to begin. Ms. Lee will clean up the lunch area and set out the planned art exploration (see lesson plan). While art exploration is in progress Ms. Lee takes her lunch break and Ms. Parks assists with afternoon nap setup.

FIGURE 3–6 Detailed Nap Schedule One

Early Afternoon	Follow the same instructions outlined for morning nap time. This nap is about 1 hour. Once Ms. Lee returns, she and Ms. Parks cover my lunch break. I update all the charts, paperwork, and notes home for the day. During my scheduled planning time on Friday, I update my lesson plans, bulletin boards, overall paperwork. While the children are asleep Ms. Lee and Ms. Parks work on the housekeeping schedule for toys, equipment, and general. Ms. Lee goes home at 3:00 pm.
Mid Afternoon	As the children begin to awaken, Ms. Parks begins diaper changes, hand washing, and sharing time. I clean up the cots (they are assigned individually so we only clean them on Thursday) (see sanitation procedures if it is Thursday). As we complete each diaper change we begin snack time. If we are running late we combine our efforts. It is our intention not to expect the toddlers to wait if they are all up and ready. Snack time begins & diaper changes continue until complete.
Late Afternoon	We begin inside play chosen from the KIDEX activity list. Ms. Parks assists with the activities. We form two small groups rather than one large group of 10. Mark and Sydney often prefer to slide and climb. We do not expect all the children to participate unless they are interested. Erica likes to sit in the high chair and read her books. Be sure to secure the safety straps. Mr. Kish arrives about 15 min before I leave. I look over final charts and he begins diaper changes, hand washing, and sharing time. During this time an assessment is made of their overall appearance. The children are changed into fresh clothing if their clothes are excessively soiled. We begin to gather items to send home.
Early Evening	Around 5:00-5:15 the children are placed around the tables and high chairs and fed a predinner snack. It usually consists of a few crackers or cheese cubes and a small sippy cup of water. We then work on fine motor activities (see lesson plan) about 10 minutes. As the children begin to depart play music, rock them, and read stories. Remind the families to check their mailboxes and events board. Send home the toddler daily sheet. When all the children have departed, disinfect the tables and finish disinfecting the soiled toys. Straighten the room for tomorrow, vacuum, and mop. Turn off the lights. Pat yourself on the back for a job well done!

Figure 3–6 Detailed Nap Schedule One *(Continued)*

DAILY TODDLER SCHEDULE DETAILS
Nap Schedule-Two

Early Morning	Ms. Golden arrives, opens the room, does a safety check of environment, and sets up play activities chosen from KIDEX; see lesson plans in KIDEX Class Book. She welcomes each child as they arrive. Ethan is new and is still experiencing separation anxiety. He calms down if he is able to wave goodbye to his mom while watching her from the window.
	The breakfast cart arrives by 7:00. Jack, Lisa, Charmaine, and Paul are the breakfast eaters. All others eat before they arrive. See Jack's individual profile KIDEX to review his food allergies. I arrive around 7:45. While Ms. Golden completes the breakfast schedule I give any medications and supervise the play center activities. Around 8:45 we begin our cleanup. Ms. Golden begins diaper changes, one-on-one sharing time, and hand washing. While she is doing that I turn on our exercise music and dance or play toddler circle games (see lesson plans in KIDEX).
Mid Morning	Snacks are served — only Timothy needs a cup with a lid. The children retrieve their blankets and nap toys for a short rest—about 15 min. We turn on soft music. Harriet and Carter will settle in if their backs are rubbed. Ethan takes a pacifier. Lisa and Paul sometimes fall asleep!
	After resting we help put away blankets and nap toys. Ms. Golden conducts the art activity with 4 or 5 children and I work with the.
	other half of the group exploring language enrichment skills—See our lesson plans (KIDEX book).
Late Morning	We clean up our art center and prepare for outdoor play (about 25–30 min). If the weather does not permit, see alternative gross motor activities on lesson plans. Upon arrival back to our room, encourage all the children to hang their outdoor coats and hats in their cubbies with assistance. Mr. Kurtz joins us and relieves Ms. Golden for lunch. Mr. Kurtz begins the diaper changing, sharing time, and hand washing. I disinfect the table and set the children at the lunch table, put on bibs, and sing songs with them. Ethan sits in the high chair with safety straps still since he is new and used to this routine at home.
Mid Day	The lunch cart arrives about 11:30 and we serve lunch. While the lunch is in progress I sit and eat a small plate of food with the children and Mr. Kurtz prepares the room for nap. As each child finishes lunch, we clean their hands and faces. They retrieve their blankets and soft nap toys. Remember Ethan's pacifier. Turn on soft music and rub Harriet and Carter's backs. The children will nap around 2 hours. Ms Golden joins Mr. Kurtz to help settle the nappers and I catch up charting. Then I take my lunch while the children sleep. Once I return from lunch I have about 1 hour prep time to work on my bulletin boards, lesson plans, and written communications. Ms. Golden and Mr. Kurtz clean up the lunch area and tend to toy cleansing and housekeeping responsibilities.

FIGURE 3–7 Detailed Nap Schedule Two

Early Afternoon	Ms. Golden goes home. We say goodbye. As the children begin to awaken around 2:30, I begin diaper changes, sharing time, and hand washing. Mr. Kurtz disinfects the cots and assists the children to put their blankets and nap toys away. Note: we keep the soft music on and the lights low (shades are opened) to allow the children to waken with ease and join back into the group. Once we are ready for snacks we turn on the overhead lights and turn off our nap music.
Mid Afternoon	As we complete the diaper changes we serve snacks to those who are ready. Once snacks are completed we go outdoors for about 30 min.
Late Afternoon	Once again indoors we put away outdoor coats and hats and begin our chosen KIDEX activities. I watch half the group while Mr. Kurtz supervises play centers / self-directed activities about 15 min, then we switch. Mr. Kurtz begins the final diaper changes, sharing time, and hand washing and changes any clothing that is extremely soiled. Ms McNabb, our floating assistant caregiver, arrives about 15 min before I leave. She begins a flannel board story or reading / vocabulary cards while I review the final charting notes.
Early Evening	I leave and she will give the toddlers a mini snack while Mr. Kurtz finishes diapers. She will stay with Mr. Kurtz until only five toddlers remain. Mr. Kurtz reminds the parents to pick up their mail and assists with departures. He prepares the room for closing and tomorrow's activities.

FIGURE 3–7 Detailed Nap Schedule Two *(Continued)*

DAILY TODDLER SCHEDULE DETAILS

At first look, the Daily Toddler Schedule Details might seem overwhelmingly busy, and one might wonder how one teacher can accomplish all the outlined tasks. Yet in reality, the child/staff ratio maintained in many programs is 5/1 or 6/1. Brendekamp and Copple in *Developmentally Appropriate Practice* (1997) advise "the maximum size for a toddler group is twelve, with one adult for no more than six toddlers, preferably fewer" (p. 690). The group always works more efficiently with at least two adults. Working in tandem, they can manage the schedule. For instance, while one teacher performs diaper changes and sharing time, the other teacher can oversee activities such as table activities, flannel board stories, or nap time cleanup with the other children.

Use the Daily Toddler Schedule Details examples (Figures 3–6 and 3–7) to review and create your own individualized group schedule using the Daily Toddler Schedule Details blank template located in the Forms and Templates appendix. Explain in detail where equipment or specific items are stored, such as art supplies and extra clothing. Paint a complete picture of every component listed on the daily schedule. Once a substitute has reviewed the Daily Toddler Schedule Outline he or she can refer to the Daily Toddler Schedule Details to recreate a routine the children are familiar with, thus promoting the stable, secure feeling toddlers need to thrive.

INTRODUCE US TO YOUR TODDLER

Upon enrolling a toddler in the center program, provide the parents or guardians with an Introduce Us to Your Toddler sheet (Figure 3–8). This form provides the families a means for familiarizing the center staff with the needs and requirements of each individual toddler. Because every toddler will change rapidly, it is advisable to update each child's personal information on a monthly basis. After the first month of attendance, replace the original document called Introduce Us to Your Toddler with the Toddlers Individual Monthly Profile provided in Figure 3–9.

KIDEX FOR TODDLERS INDIVIDUAL MONTHLY PROFILE

The Toddlers Individual Monthly Profile is one of the most important documents for providing a map of each child's individual preferences and needs. The Toddlers Individual Monthly Profile is an in-house document intended for in-house communication among the staff. Because toddlers have limited language skills, they are not able to communicate their needs effectively. They are not able to communicate if they have a food allergy or they wear a diaper only at nap time. By creating and maintaining a current copy of the Toddlers Individual Monthly Profile for each child, caregivers can ensure those important details are not overlooked.

Record personality traits you have observed. Circle all that apply. Mark the level of assistance needed with regard to dietary patterns. Young toddlers will require assistance learning to nourish themselves. They have not yet mastered the use of utensils and sometimes, if they are tired from an active play period, they will not be up to completing the task without assistance. Note if they have any food dislikes. Young children are very sensitive to taste and often reject newly introduced flavors, yet grow to love them at a later time, so their food likes and dislikes may change on a regular basis.

Introduce Us to Your Toddler
(12 – 36 Months)

Date ___2/16___

Last Name: _(Enter Last Name)_ First Name: ___Jason___ Middle: ___W___

Name your child is called at home: ___Jay___

Siblings' Names & Ages: ___Beth, 5, & Raymond, 6___

Favorite Play Materials: ___clay, paint, crayons___

Special Interests: ___dinosaurs___

Pets: ___dog (Rusty), cat (Charlie)___

What opportunities does your child have to play with others the same age? ___Sunday school, Mommy-and-me classes___

Eating Patterns:

 Are there any dietary concerns? ___Picky eater___

 Does your child feed himself or herself? ___Yes___

 Are there any food dislikes? ___Milk___

 Are there any food allergies? ___no___

 When eating, uses fingers ___ spoon _X_ fork _X_ needs assistance _sometimes_

Sleeping Patterns:

 What time is bedtime at home? ___7:30___ Arise at? ___6:00___

 What time is nap time? ___2:00___ How long? _2 hours_

 Does your child have a special toy/blanket to nap with? ___Purple dinosoar___

 How is your child prepared for rest (e.g., story time, quiet play, snack)
 ___Story or soft music___

Eliminating Patterns:

 Not potty trained yet? ___yes___ (skip to health patterns)

 In training? _____ If trained, how long? _____

 Independent–doesn't require help. _____

 Does your child need to be reminded? ___yes___

 If yes, at what time intervals? ___every 1.5 hours___

 Does your child have certain words to indicate a need to eliminate? _"go potty"_
 "go pee pee"

Child wears:

 Nap time diaper ___X___ Disposable training pants _____

 Cloth underwear ___X___ Plastic pants over cloth underwear ___X___

Figure 3–8 Introduce Us to Your Toddler

Stress/Coping Patterns:

Uses pacifier _____ Brand_____

Does your child have any fears: _____ Storms _____ Separation anxiety ____

Dark _____ Animals _____ Stranger anxiety _____*x*_____

Being alone _____ Other _____

How do you soothe him or her? *Hugs, or redirect him to a book or dinosaur*

Health Patterns:

List any medications, intervals, and route (mouth, ears, eyes, etc.):

_____*none*_____

List any health issues or special needs: _____*none*_____

_____

Activity Patterns:

When did your child begin: Creeping *5 months* Crawling *6 months* Walking *11 months*

Indicate your child's symptoms when teething. *Runny nose, fussy*_____

_____

Is there any other information we should know in order to help us know your child better?

Loves to be tickled, sometimes doesn't like to share, loves to sing and dance

_____

_____

Other Comments: _____

_____

_____

_____*Mrs. Marsh*_____

Parent/Guardian completing form

OFFICE USE ONLY

Start Date: _____ Full Time: _____ Part Time: S M T W T F S ½ a.m. p.m.

Group Assigned: a.m. _____ p.m. _____

Caregiver(s): _____

Please keep an adjustment record for _____ weeks.

Assign a cubby space: _____ Assign a diaper space: _____

FIGURE 3–8 Introduce Us to Your Toddler *(Continued)*

KIDEX for Toddlers
Individual Monthly Profile

Month: __Nov.__   Caregivers: __Ms. Smith, Ms. Reynolds__

Child's Name: __Alberto__   Group: __Blueberries__

Age: __1.5__   Birth Date: __2-13-2003__   Allergies: __none__

Parents'/Guardians' Names: __Manuel and Barbara__   Start Date: __Nov. 5__

Special Blanket/Toy: __robot__   Pacifier Type: __binky__

Diapers: __X__   Nap time Diaper Only: _____   *Potty Trained: _____
* The majority of toddlers potty train at ages 2½ –3 years
Independent: _____   Needs reminding: _____   Potty training: __no__

Special Diapering Instructions (special ointments, etc): __none__

Personality Traits: shy/reserved   outgoing/curious   sensitive/frightens easily
(Circle all that apply)   very verbal   active   ~~restless~~
    (cuddly)   demonstrative   (stranger anxiety)
    cautious

Dietary Patterns: needs help _____   uses spoon/fork independently __X__

Food Dislikes: __fish, cheese__

Health Concerns: __asthma__

Daily Medications: yes __X__   no _____   (see med sheet for details)

Special Needs Instructions: __On humid days he can't go outside.__

Stress/Coping Pattern: fears _____   storms _____   loudness _____   strangers _____
    dark _____   animals __X__   separation anxiety _____   others _____

Number of Naps: (1) or 2   Average Nap Length: AM _____   PM __2 hours__

Special Nap Instructions: __Alberto must have his pacifier and robot__
__before he can fall asleep.__

Favorite Activities This Month: __riding scooter!__

Days Attending: Sun.   (Mon.)   Tues.   (Wed.)   Thurs.   (Fri.)   Sat.   1/2 days   (Full days)

Approximate Arrival Time __7:30__   Approximate Departure Time __5:15__

Those authorized to pick up: __parents, grandparents__

Warning: If name is not listed, consult with office and obtain permission to release child. If you are not familiar with this person, always request I.D.

FIGURE 3–9 Toddlers Individual Monthly Profile

If a child is using a spoon or fork without difficulty, then indicate he or she is independent. List any health concerns or indicate "none known." The daily medications line requires only a no or yes. This line includes a reminder to check the current daily group medication sheet.

Some children will have special needs, such as to remove leg braces for 30 minutes in the morning and afternoon. It is common for some toddlers to be frightened of loud or unfamiliar noises such as fire alarms, vacuum cleaners, and thunderstorms. Yet others never seem to notice. Indicate any fears under stress/coping pattern.

Young toddlers (12–15 months) generally fare best with a two-nap schedule in a busy child care setting. Mark on the sheet how many naps children are accustomed to and include their average length, though these will vary with the child's needs. Toddlers thrive on ritual and will appreciate consistent nap time routines. Describe all details such as "rests best with soft yellow duck and gentle patting."

Favorite activities will change from month to month but are very important to toddlers as they practice skills over and over. Indicate all you are aware of in this section.

Finish the Toddlers Individual Monthly Profile marking the days the child is scheduled to attend, half days or full days, and approximate arrival and departure times. It is extremely crucial to document and abide by who is authorized to pick up the child. See "Authorized Person Card" later in this chapter for a more in-depth discussion of how to facilitate authorized pickup procedures. In this section of the Toddlers Individual Monthly Profile, provide a list of authorized people for the substitute teachers to refer to. Make it a solid policy to consult with the administrative office if a person is not listed and to always I.D. any unfamiliar person.

APPLICATION FOR ENROLLING A TODDLER

Use this application to begin building an administrative file for each new child. Note that this document is different from Introduce Us to Your Toddler. The application is generally stored in the administrative offices with permanent health records and legal documents. Items to include on an application for collecting general information are

- infant's name, address, home phone number, date of birth, gender, legal guardian
- mother's name, address, home phone number, cell phone, e-mail, employer's name, work phone number
- father's name, address, home phone number, cell phone, e-mail, employer's name, work phone number
- emergency contact's name, relationship, address, home phone number, work phone number
- name of other people residing with the child, their relationship, age (if under 21)
- names of all people authorized to remove the child from the center, relationships
- days the child will attend, full or part time
- medical emergency information and authorization
- permission to leave the center for neighborhood walks, bus ride to and from center, and so on (see Figure 3–10).

PROGRAM ENROLLING APPLICATION

Child's Full Name: _Susan (Enter Last Name)_   Nickname: _Sue_

Date of Birth: _9-2-2004_   Sex: _F_   Home Phone: _XXX-XXX-XXXX_

Address: _(Enter Street #)_   City: _(Enter City)_   Zip Code: _(Enter Zip Code)_

Legal Guardian: _mother & father_

Mother's Name: _Laura_   Home Phone: _XXX-XXX-XXXX_

Cell Phone: _XXX-XXX-XXXX_ E-mail: _(Enter E-mail)_

Address: _same_   City: _(Enter City)_   Zip Code: _(Enter Zip Code)_

Employer: _Community Resources_   Work Phone: _XXX-XXX-XXXX_

Address: _(Enter Street #/Apt. #)_   City: _(Enter City)_   Zip Code: _(Enter Zip Code)_

Father's Name: _Robert_   Home Phone: _XXX-XXX-XXXX_

Cell Phone: _XXX-XXX-XXXX_ E-mail: _(Enter E-mail)_

Address: _(Enter Street #/Apt. #)_   City: _(Enter City)_   Zip Code: _(Enter Zip Code)_

Employer: _Technical Facilities_   Work Phone: _XXX-XXX-XXXX_

Address: _(Enter Street #/Apt. #)_   City: _(Enter City)_   Zip Code: _(Enter Zip Code)_

IN THE EVENT YOU CANNOT BE REACHED IN AN EMERGENCY, CALL:

Name: _Robert_   Relationship: _Father_   Phone: _XXX-XXX-XXXX_

Address: _same_   City: _____   Zip Code: _____

Name: _Ellie_   Relationship: _Grandmother_ Phone: _XXX-XXX-XXXX_

Address: _(Enter Street #)_   City: _(Enter City)_   Zip Code: _(Enter Zip Code)_

OTHER PEOPLE RESIDING WITH CHILD

Name: _Lilly_   Relationship: _Sister_   Age: _7_

Name: _____   Relationship: _____   Age: _____

Name: _____   Relationship: _____   Age: _____

PEOPLE AUTHORIZED TO REMOVE CHILD FROM THE CENTER

Your child will not be allowed to go with anyone unless their name appears on this application, or you provide them with an "authorization card," or you make other arrangements with the management. Positive I.D. will be required.

Name: _Laura_   Relationship: _Mother_

Name: _Robert_   Relationship: _Father_

Name: _Ellie_   Relationship: _Grandmother_

Child Will Attend: Mon - (Tues) - Wed - (Thur) - Fri - (Sat) - Sun

Figure 3–10 Program Enrolling Application

Child Will Be: (Full Time) or Part Time

Time Child Will Be Dropped Off (Normally): _7:30 am_

Time Child Will Be Picked Up (Normally): _4:45 pm_

MEDICAL INFORMATION/AUTHORIZATION

Physician's Name: _Dr. Jones_   Phone: _XXX-XXX-XXXX_

Address: _(Enter Street #)_   City: _(Enter City)_   Zip Code: _(Enter Zip Code)_

Dentist's Name: _Dr. Green_   Phone: _XXX-XXX-XXXX_

Address: _(Enter Street #)_   City: _(Enter City)_   Zip Code: _(Enter Zip Code)_

Allergies: _pollen_

I agree and give consent that, in case of accident, injury, or illness of a serious nature, my child will be given medical attention/emergency care. I understand I will be contacted immediately, or as soon as possible if I am away from the numbers listed on this form.

PERMISSION TO LEAVE PREMISES

I hereby give the school/center _Sunrise Daycare_ permission to take my child

on neighborhood walks using a _buggy_ (state equipment, e.g., a

child buggy that seats six children & has safety straps). YES_ LL _(INITIAL) NO, I

do not give permission at this time: _____ (INITIAL)

Parent/Guardian's Signature: _Laura (Enter Last Name)_

Parent/Guardian's Signature: _Robert (Enter Last Name)_

Date: _11-6_

FIGURE 3–10 Program Enrolling Application *(Continued)*

IMMUNIZATIONS

To protect all children attending the center, medical authorities suggest they all have current immunizations. Since the recommended dosages and types of immunizations continually fluctuate, you can refer to the American Academy of Pediatrics Web site (http://www.aap.org) or your local health department for the most recent schedule. Sometimes a center encounters children who do not have current immunizations for a variety of reasons such as medical conditions or religious preferences. If immunizations are withheld for any reason, collect in writing from the parent or legal guardian, the child's physician, and/or religious leader the specific reason and keep it in the child's record. This written documentation will provide state licensing representatives support for lack of immunization records. Special care should be taken to notify and exclude underimmunized children from the program if an active vaccine-preventable disease occurs in the facility.

AUTHORIZED PERSON CARD

The enrolling application template mentions "authorization cards" (see Figure 3–11) under "People Authorized to Remove Child from the Center." Consider using authorization cards for those occasions when parents/guardians are unable to remove their child from the center due to unforeseen circumstances. They might need to depend on a substitute such as a coworker, neighbor, or family member not listed on the authorized list. Upon enrollment, provide the family with a couple of blank authorization cards. Instruct them to complete one and call the center to give verbal permission and provide the name of the person who will call for the child. Some states require a code number or word to accompany the authorized person. Check your local licensing agency for specific password mandates. When the substitute person arrives, request a picture I.D. to verify that the name matches the one on the authorization card. Collect the card and return it to the parents on their next visit to the center.

HOW TO CREATE A CURRENT EVENTS BULLETIN BOARD

A Current Events Bulletin Board provides a centrally located place to post messages. It is an important center for communication between the program, current participating families, and future families touring your facility. In a busy toddler room time is of the essence. The Current Events Bulletin Board will save busy teachers from the repetition of repeating

USE HEAVY CARD STOCK (FRONT OF CARD)   **USE HEAVY CARD STOCK (BACK OF CARD)**

FIGURE 3–11 Authorization Card (Front & Back)

information to each individual family and reduces the chance information will not be disseminated to everyone. Look at Figure 3–5 for an example of the Current Events Bulletin Board.

Decorate the bulletin board with a seasonal theme so you don't have to spend time changing it more than a few times a year. All you will need to change are the daily and monthly communication pieces. Hang the bulletin board near the room entrance where everyone passes by. If it is located at the back of the room, chances are busy parents won't take the opportunity to read it every day. The following are suggested items to post on the class Current Events Bulletin Board. Add items you feel are vital to your room's operation.

Daily Toddler Schedule Outline:	Use this area to post the general schedule for the group.
Birthdays:	Post the birth date of each child. If space is limited on the bulletin board, dedicate a space in your room.
Future Events:	Here is a great place to post future events: for example, a scheduled visit from "Charlie," the pet pig.
Toddler News:	Post current events such as who has a new tooth, or family news (a new baby sister is on the way!).
Health News:	Choose articles from Chapter 8 to explain a recent exposure to a communicable disease and what symptoms to watch for.
Nutrition & Menu Information:	Post a copy of your menu for the day, week, or month. Many families find this information helpful for planning home meals that complement the center's meals. Refer to Figure 3-12 for an example of a daily menu.
Parent Articles:	Post information relevant to toddlers, such as "How Children Learn Empathy," or a schedule of parenting classes offered in the community.
Calendars & Center Newsletter:	If your center creates a monthly newsletter or calendar, post current copies here. Find examples of both in Figures 3-13 and 3-14.
Allergy Postings:	Post a listing indicating the child's name and known allergies. Collect this information from the Toddlers Individual Monthly Profile.

TODDLER DAILY OBSERVATION CHECKLISTS

Toddlers are unable to discuss their daily activities with their families. Accurate recording provides the family with a clear picture of that day. Figure 3–15 provides a completed example of a Toddler Daily Observation Checklist.

Consider producing the Toddler Daily Observation Checklists using two-part forms. Provide one copy for the parents or guardians at departure. File the second copy for two to three months, keeping at least the past two months at all times. Your local licensing agency might require a longer period of storage.

It is very helpful to have written observation documents to review when a family conference is warranted. Occasionally parents express concerns. For example, they might be concerned their child's appetite seems to be fluctuating at home and want to explore how their child's appetite compares at the center. A series of daily sheets will help track any unusual patterns the toddler might be exhibiting. Information will provide helpful specifics needed to answer their questions. The director or program manager is encouraged to review

---

OUR MENU TODAY

Thursday, July 6

Breakfast	Milk 2% (½ cup)
	Apricot halves
	French toast (½ slice)
	Margarine (1 tsp)
	Syrup (1 tsp)
Snack	Cheese (½ oz)
	Apple juice 100% Vitamin C (¼ cup)
	Crackers (½ serving/0.5 oz)
Lunch	Milk 2% (½ cup)
	Baked chicken (½ oz)
	Diced mixed vegetables (¼ cup)
	Fruit cocktail (¼ cup)
Snack	Blueberry yogurt (2 oz)
	Graham crackers (1 square)
	Water (2–4 oz)
Mini Snack	Saltines (2 squares)
	Water (2–4 oz)

Figure 3–12 Menu Example

all records at least monthly to look for consistent recording practices or spot areas where intervention on a matter is warranted.

NOTES HOME/STAFF COLLABORATION

The director is responsible for the overall well-being of the staff, parents, and children. The director must be kept informed of any unusual changes, challenges, or problems that might occur during the course of the shift. It can be very disconcerting for a director to be completely uninformed when an emotionally upset client approaches him or her. Discuss any written communication with the director prior to sending notes home, other than a note to request personal supplies or each child's daily record. After discussing the problem at hand you can devise a shared plan of action. Sharing your concerns with the director will facilitate problem solving as well as keep him or her continually informed. The director may have encountered a similar situation before and have a workable solution.

FRAGILE PARENT RELATIONSHIPS

Experienced early care and education professionals are well aware that newly enrolled families are most "fragile" within the first several weeks of their child's attendance. For some parents this is the first time they have been separated from their child for any length of time. They might experience sadness, anxiety, and feelings of guilt. This is a hand-holding stage as a trusting relationship is established. Once we become familiar

CLASS NEWSLETTER

Enriching the Lives of Children Since 1979

TODDLER HIGHLIGHTS

Raspberries
Ms. Bluebell & Ms. Arnold

Our summer has been great so far! We have been playing outside a lot. We are so excited about our swimming time every Monday.

Alex loves to paint pretty pictures. Maybe he will be a famous artist someday.

Hannah is a real entertainer. She loves to show people her silly antics.

Laura is our biggest helper during clean-up time. Thank you, Laura.

Amanda has adjusted so well to the Raspberry room. She has made lots of new friends and loves to dance with all of them.

Danielle is such a big girl. She loves to sit and look at books.

Madalyn is developing quite a vocabulary. Her favorite word is "ball."

Megan is our "outdoorsy" girl. She especially loves the slide.

John Andrew gives great hugs. He is our loving boy.

Blueberries
Ms. Calico, Ms. Brown, Ms. Neihoff

The Blueberries give a BIG WELCOME to Sarah, Lisa, Jimmy, and Danika. Sarah and Lisa are both newcomers to the center, while Jimmy and Danika just moved up from the Raspberry group.

Alex has been visiting with the Banana group this week. She will be ready to move up soon.

Alexander loves riding on the toy airplane. Sometimes he wants to fly it home.

Niki has the most vibrant laughter that delights all of us.

Madalyn shares her dimpled smile often when she is playing with her friends.

Evan is so proud of showing everyone that he can walk around and go any place he wants.

Mackenzie loves to sing all the time. She keeps going for that high note.

Maggie adores climbing and sliding on the playground equipment.

Erin is one of the leaders of the group. She leads her friends around the room laughing and singing.

Kathryn has a way of making you smile when you are feeling blue.

FIGURE 3–13 Class Newsletter

CLASS CALENDAR

July

Sunday	Monday	Tuesday	Wednesday	Thursday	Friday	Saturday
						1
2 Center theme: *Yankee Doodle*	3	4 Center closed: Happy Birthday America	5	6 6:00 First Aid Class	7 Happy Birthday Jennifer	8
9 Center theme: *Down on the Farm*	10 *Fire drill practice this week*	11 Happy Birthday Sean	12 Happy Birthday Ronnie 6:00 Lead Teacher Mtg	13 Preschool & Jr. K Bring a t-shirt to paint for the zoo trip	14	15 Happy Birthday Erin
16 Center theme: *Let's Go to the Zoo*	17	18 Center Zoo: Everyone bring your favorite zoo stuffed animal	19 Grapes, Apples, and Plums go to the zoo	20	21	22
23 Center theme: *Under the Sea*	24	25 Merry Christmas in July	26 7:00 Parents Round Table	27 Happy Birthday Michael & Katie	28 Happy Birthday Ian	29
30 Center theme: *Lost in Space*	31 Happy Birthday Patrick					

Figure 3–14 Class Calendar

Toddler Daily Observation Checklist

Child's name: _____Ethan_____ Date: _1/27/2005_
Arrival: _____7:30 am_____ Departure: ____5:00 pm____

	Ate Partial	Ate Complete	Oz. Formula
Breakfast		✓	
Snack	✓		
Lunch	✓		8 oz
Snack		✓	
Mini Snack		✓	
Dinner		Home	
Evening Snack			

	Medications *	Treatments *
Time	8:00 am Eye drops	None
Time	12:30 pm Eye drops	None
Time	4:45 pm	Asthma Treatment

* see daily medication sheets for details

Diaper Changes				
Time	Wet	BM	Dry	Initials
9:00 a	✓	✓		A.C.
11:00 a	✓			K.S.
1:45 p	✓			K.S.
4:15 p			✓	L.P.

Nap Times: _9:30 – 10:50 am_   _2:00 – 3:00 pm_   Other: _____

Potty Training Progress					
Time	Wet	Dry	Bowel Movement	Accident Clothing Change	Seemed confused upset/resisted/refused re-evaluate readiness

Moods / Activity Level:
Circle all that apply
Busy • (Curious) •
Adventurous •
Active • (Cheerful) •
Quiet • Content •
Cuddly • Drowsy •
Bubbly • (Verbal) •
Defiant • Focused
• Frustrated Easily

Today's Play Center Choices: ___Library Books___   ___Popper Toys / Sliding___

Comments: _____Aunt Mary dropped by at lunchtime. Ethan was delighted!_____

Lead Caregiver: ___Mrs. Carlyle___
Shift Time: _8 – 5_
Caregiver: ___Ms. Strom___
Shift Time: _6:30 – 3:30_
Caregiver: ___Ms. Applebaum___
Shift Time: _____
Caregiver: ___Mr. Patel___
Shift Time: _3:00 – 6:00_
Caregiver: _____
Shift Time: _____

FIGURE 3–15 Toddler Daily Observation Checklist

with our routines it is easy to forget how it feels to be new to the center setting. Offer them information about the daily routines or invite them to visit before their child's first day at the center. Challenge yourself to look at each new family and recollect how you felt on your first day.

It is imperative to establish trust and rapport quickly. New parents appreciate an extra big welcome in the morning, and it is your responsibility to include them in discussions while establishing care. Show them where to store their child's belongings, where to sign in for the day, and where they can find the child's daily sheets. Introduce them to other parents so they begin to feel a part of the group quickly. As rapport builds, a level of trust will begin to develop and they will naturally settle into a familiar, comfortable routine.

Another time a client might be considered fragile is when an upsetting situation occurs involving their child. If families do not feel the staff views their concerns as legitimate, their trust is compromised. Some fairly common scenarios are if a recently healthy child now is experiencing frequent bouts of illnesses, if a child isn't getting along with another child, or if there is a child that bites in the group. Again, this is a time to make an extra effort to reassure the family that you are sympathetic to their concerns and committed to resolving the problem. Share more information to assist their understanding. If a situation can be improved, outline what plan of action you have put into place to correct the situation or prevent it from recurring.

Sometimes the concerns do not involve classroom situations. For example, they may experience an error with their billing or dislike how their billing has been handled. Because parents naturally bond with classroom teachers through positive daily contact, sometimes they feel more comfortable sharing their concerns with the classroom personnel rather than with administrative personnel. At times they may experience some dissatisfaction in other center matters. If you hear a parent voicing a concern, it is very helpful to share this observation with the director. It provides an opportunity to proactively alleviate any misunderstandings or clear up whatever frustrations the client may be experiencing. It takes a whole team to make child care a pleasant and positive experience for everyone, and it is very important to keep the lines of communication open on all levels. Managers, with their vast array of experience, can often smooth out matters and reach mutually accepted outcomes quickly.

REFERENCES

Bredekamp, S., & Copple, C. (1997). *Developmentally appropriate practice.* Washington, DC: National Association for the Education of Young Children.

Reisser, P. C. M. (1997). *Baby & child care.* Carol Stream, IL: Tyndale House.

RECOMMENDED RESOURCES

Caring for our children: National health & safety performance standards (2nd ed.). http://www.ncr.edu

High/Scope Educational Research Foundation, http://www.highscope.org

Jurek, D. (1995). *Teaching young children.* Morristown, NJ: Fearon Teacher Aids.

Shelov, S.P., MD, FAAP, & Hannemann, R.E., MD, FAAP. *Caring for your baby and young child: Birth to age 5* (4th ed.). American Academy of Pediatrics, http://www.aap.org

To find your specific
State's Licensing, Rules
and Regulations go to:

http://nrc.uchsc.edu

Hygiene, Cleaning, and Disinfecting

CHAPTER 4

Proper cleaning, disinfecting, and hygiene practices employed consistently in an early care and teaching environment will significantly reduce the spread of infection and disease. Disinfecting and cleaning are two distinctly different procedures used to prevent the spread of germs and require their own specific measures to achieve their intended results. *Cleaning* is a *less* rigorous procedure and is designed to remove dirt, soil, and small amounts of bacteria. It *does not eliminate all germs*. Soap, detergents, and cleaners are examples of cleaning products. *Disinfecting* procedures are *more* rigorous and refer to cleaning surfaces with the use of chemicals, *virtually eliminating all germs*. Diaper tables are an example of a place where disinfecting procedures are employed. In order for a disinfectant solution to work effectively, the instructions must be adhered to. Disinfecting products require a certain concentration of solution and must remain in contact with the contaminated item for a specific period of time. The Environmental Protection Agency (EPA) regulates the use of disinfectants. To avoid confusing a cleaning agent with a disinfecting agent, look at the label. Products that are capable of disinfecting will bear an EPA approval on the label.

If you are mixing your own disinfecting solutions, the National Health and Safety Performance Standards for Child Care recommends ¼ cup of bleach in 1 gallon of water. Mix fresh daily. To avoid creating a poisonous gas, never mix bleach with anything other than water.

Chlorine bleach solutions have been known to aggravate asthma or other respiratory conditions. Some care providers are concerned with the potential toxic effects of common household products used abundantly in an early care environment. There are several effective natural disinfecting products on the market. Check your local health food stores for a variety of products or check in the recommended resources section at the end of this chapter.

DIAPER CHANGING PROCEDURES

Frequent diaper changing ensures a toddler's comfort and prevents skin irritations. Check each child's diaper status upon arrival. Toddlers require a diaper change at least four times during an eight- to nine-hour shift. Absolute cleanliness during diaper changes is of primary importance. Do not change diapers on surfaces that come in close contact with children during play, such as couches, floor areas where children play, and so on. Many viruses and infections are easily spread from child to child. A disease can be carried by people who are completely without symptoms and passed on to others causing severe diarrhea to the point of dehydration, hospitalization, and lengthy illness. Employing the procedures outlined in Figure 4–1 for disposable diaper changes and Figure 4–2 for cloth diaper changes will help ensure you and the little ones will remain healthy.

Diaper changing time is a wonderful opportunity for sharing special one-on-one moments. This is a repetitive routine performed many times a day. This is a great opportunity to visit one-on-one and talk about things the toddler is experiencing in his or

Diaper Changing Procedures for Disposable Diapers

Supplies: Disposable nonabsorbent gloves, nonabsorbent paper liner, disposable wipes removed from container, child's personally labeled ointments (under medical direction), diapers, cotton balls, plastic bags, tissues, physician-prescribed lotions, lidded hands-free plastic-lined trash container, soap, disinfectant, and paper towels.

Use a nonabsorbent changing surface. Avoid dangerous falls: keep a hand on baby at all times and never leave alone. In emergency, put child on floor or take with you.

	Steps for Changing Disposable Diapers				
1	Wash hands with soap and water.	2	Gather supplies.	3	Put on disposable waterproof gloves (if used).
4	Cover diapering surface with nonabsorbent paper liner.	5	Place baby on prepared diapering area (minimize contact: hold baby away from your body if extremely wet or soiled).	6	Put soiled clothes in a plastic bag.
7	Unfasten diaper. Leave soiled diaper under the child.	8	Gently wash baby's bottom. Remove stool and urine from front to back, and use a fresh wipe each time. Dispose directly in designated receptacle.	9	Fold soiled diaper inward and place in designated receptacle followed by the disposable gloves (if used).
10	Use disposable wipe to clean surface of caregiver's hands and another to clean the child's.	11	Check for spills on paper. If present, fold over so fresh part is under buttocks.	12	Place clean diaper under baby.
13	Using a cotton ball or tissue, apply skin ointment to clean, dry area if indicated/ordered.	14	Fasten diaper and dress with fresh clothing.	15	Wash baby's hands with soap and water between 60° and 120°F for 15-20 seconds and dry. Turn faucet off with paper towel, then place baby in a safe location.
16	Clean and disinfect diapering area, leaving bleach solution in contact at least 2 minutes. Allow table to air dry, or wipe it after 2 minutes.	17	Wash your hands with soap and water for at least 15–20 seconds. Turn off faucet with paper towel.	18	Chart diaper change and any observations.

Adopted from: Standard 3.014 Diaper Changing Procedure. Caring for Our Children, National health and safety performance standards (2nd ed.) Used with permission, American Academy of Pediatrics.

FIGURE 4–1 Diaper Changing Procedures for Disposable Diapers

Diaper Changing Procedures for Cloth Diapers

Supplies: Disposable nonabsorbent gloves, nonabsorbent paper liner, disposable wipes removed from container, child's personally labeled ointments (under medical direction), diapers, cotton balls, plastic bags, tissues, physician-prescribed lotions, lidded hands-free plastic-lined trash container, soap, disinfectant, and paper towels.

Soiled Diapers: *Contain in a labeled and washable plastic-lined receptacle that is tightly lidded and hands-free only. Don't require separate bags. However, any soiled diapers sent home are to be secured in a plastic bag, separately bagged from soiled clothing. Clean and disinfect receptacle daily and dispose of waste water in toilet or floor drain only.*

Use a nonabsorbent changing surface. Avoid dangerous falls: keep a hand on baby at all times and never leave alone. In emergency, put child on floor or take with you.

				**Steps for Changing Cloth Diapers**				

1	Wash hands with liquid soap and water.	2	Gather supplies.	3	Put on disposable waterproof gloves (if used).
4	Cover diapering surface with nonabsorbent paper liner.	5	Place baby on prepared diapering area (minimize contact: hold baby away from your body if extremely wet or soiled).	6	Put soiled clothes in a plastic bag.
7	Unfasten diaper. Leave soiled diaper under the child. Close each safety pin immediately out of child's reach. Never hold pins in mouth.	8	Gently wash baby's bottom. Remove stool and urine from front to back, and use a fresh wipe each time. Dispose directly in designated receptacle.	9	Fold soiled diaper inward and place in designated receptacle followed by the disposable gloves (if used).
10	Use disposable wipe to clean surface of caregiver's hands and another to clean the child's.	11	Check for spills on paper. If procent, fold over so fresh part is under buttocks.	12	Place clean diaper under baby.
13	Using a cotton ball or tissue, apply skin ointment to clean, dry area if indicated/ordered.	14	Fasten diaper with pins, placing your hand between the child and the diaper on insertion, and dress with fresh clothing.	15	Wash baby's hands with soap and water between 60° and 120°F for 15-20 seconds and dry. Turn faucet off with paper towel, then place baby in a safe location.
16	Clean and disinfect diapering area, leaving bleach solution in contact at least 2 minutes. Allow table to air dry, or wipe it after 2 minutes.	17	Wash your hands with soap and water for at least 15–20 seconds. Turn off faucet with paper towel.	18	Chart diaper change and any observations.

Adopted from: Standard 3.014 Diaper Changing Procedure. Caring for Our Children, National health and safety performance standards (2nd ed.) Used with permission, American Academy of Pediatrics.

FIGURE 4–2 Diaper Changing Procedures for Cloth Diapers

her day. Meaningful experiences with the child could be missed if care is not taken to be fully present during this time. Use this occasion to listen, talk, or sing with each toddler. Describe your actions, such as: "Grace, let's change your diaper. You love to have your diaper changed. A dry diaper will feel so nice!" Plan specific "sharing time" subjects to discuss with the toddler, or choose interesting pictures to keep in the diapering area and change them often. Post them near the diaper changing table for all staff to use. Diaper changing can be a very vulnerable time for children, and how we treat them communicates our attitude toward them. They will develop feelings of acceptance and security in a kind and respectful climate.

The suggested diaper changing equipment and details for creating a diaper changing area are listed in Chapter 2, "Creating and Organizing a Toddler Room." Requirements for diaper changes vary from state to state. Some areas, for instance, allow changing to occur in the toddler's personally assigned crib; others allow a choice of whether disposable gloves are used. According to Standard 3.014 Diaper Changing Procedure, *Caring for Our Children, National Health and Safety Performance Standards* (2nd ed.), the following diaper changing procedures should be posted in the changing area and shall be assessed as part of staff evaluation of caregivers who do diaper changing. Caregivers must never leave a child alone on a table or countertop, even for an instant. A safety strap or harness shall not be used on the diaper changing table. If an emergency arises, caregivers shall put the child on the floor or take the child with them.

STEP 1: Get organized. Before you bring the child to the diaper changing area, wash your hands, gather what you need, and bring it to the diaper changing table:

- nonabsorbent paper liner large enough to cover the changing surface from the child's shoulders to beyond the child's feet
- fresh diaper, clean clothes (if you need them)
- wipes for cleaning the child's genitalia and buttocks—use a pop-up dispenser or remove the wipes from the container so you will not touch the container during diaper changing
- a plastic bag for any soiled clothes
- disposable gloves, if you plan to use them (put gloves on before handling soiled clothing or diapers)
- a thick application of any diaper cream (when appropriate) removed from the container to a piece of disposable material such as facial or toilet tissue

STEP 2: Carry the child to the changing table, keeping soiled clothing away from you and any surfaces you cannot easily clean and sanitize after the change.

- Always keep a hand on the child.
- If the child's feet cannot be kept out of the diaper or from contact with soiled skin during the changing process, remove the child's shoes and socks so the child does not contaminate these surfaces with stool or urine during the diaper change.
- Put soiled clothes in a plastic bag and securely tie the plastic bag to send the soiled clothes home.

STEP 3: Clean the child's diaper area.

- Place the child on the diaper changing surface and unfasten the diaper but leave the soiled diaper under the child.
- If safety pins are used, close each pin immediately once it is removed and keep pins out of the child's reach. Never hold pins in your mouth.

- Older toddlers are very active and mobile and sometimes they would rather wrestle than have their diaper changed. A great technique that will often calm them involves giving them an object to hold and manipulate while you accomplish your mission.

- Lift the child's legs as needed to use disposable wipes to clean the skin on the child's genitalia and buttocks. Remove stool and urine from front to back, and use a fresh wipe each time. Put the soiled wipes into the soiled diaper or directly into a plastic-lined, hands-free, covered can.

STEP 4: Remove the soiled diaper without contaminating any surface not already in contact with stool or urine.

- Fold the soiled surface of the diaper inward.

- Put soiled disposable diapers in a covered, plastic-lined, hands-free, covered can. If reusable cloth diapers are used, put the soiled cloth diaper and its contents (without emptying or rinsing) in a plastic bag or into a plastic-lined, hands-free, covered can to give to the parents or laundry service.

- If gloves were used, remove them using the proper technique and put them into a plastic-lined, hands-free, covered can.

- Whether or not gloves were used, use a disposable wipe to clean the surfaces of the caregiver's hands and another to clean the child's hands, and put the wipes into the plastic-lined, hands-free, covered can.

- Check for spills under the child. If there are any, fold over the paper that extends under the child's feet so a fresh, unsoiled paper surface is now under the child's buttocks.

STEP 5: Put on a clean diaper and dress the child.

- Slide a fresh diaper under the child.

- Use a facial or toilet tissue to apply any necessary diaper creams, discarding the tissue in a plastic-lined, hands-free, covered can.

- Note and plan to report any skin problems such as redness, skin cracks, or bleeding.

- Fasten the diaper. If pins are used, place your hand between the child and the diaper when inserting the pin.

STEP 6: Wash the child's hands and return the child to a supervised area.

- Use soap and water, no less than 60°F and no more than 120°F, at a sink to wash the child's hands, if you can.

- If a child is too heavy to hold for hand washing or cannot stand at the sink, use commercial disposable diaper wipes or follow this procedure:
  - Wipe the child's hands with a damp paper towel moistened with a drop of liquid soap.
  - Wipe the child's hands with a paper towel wet with clear water.
  - Dry the child's hands with a paper towel.

STEP 7: Clean and sanitize the diaper changing surface.

- Dispose of the disposable paper liner used on the diaper changing surface in a plastic-lined, hands-free, covered can.

- Clean any visible soil from the changing surface with detergent and water; rinse with water.

■ Wet the entire changing surface with the sanitizing solution (i.e., spray a sanitizing bleach solution of ¼ cup of household liquid chlorine bleach in 1 gallon of tap water, mixed fresh daily).

■ Put away the spray bottle of sanitizer. If the recommended bleach solution is sprayed as a sanitizer on the surface, leave it in contact with the surface for at least 2 minutes. The surface can be left to air dry or can be wiped dry after 2 minutes of contact with the bleach solution.

Step 8: Wash your hands, and record the diaper change in the child's daily log.

■ Record the diaper change and detail any skin irritation, loose stools, unusual odors, blood in the stool, or elimination concerns on the Toddler's Daily Record. If you are concerned by any of your findings, share this information with the director or lead teacher.

PRACTICING DIAPER RETURN DEMONSTRATIONS

In a medical setting it is common for the personnel to employ the use of return practice demonstrations for procedures requiring sterile or hygienic techniques. Sterile and hygienic practices must be carried out in a specific order. Cutting corners by leaving out parts of a routine procedure will compromise the integrity of the hygienic practice.

Although most child care programs are not medical programs, the adoption of some of their notable practices makes sense. Diaper changing sessions consume a large part of every day in a toddler room. The very nature of repeating a task over and over can become monotonous at times, thus lending itself to a break in procedure. A breakdown in procedure will seriously compromise the hygienic practices necessary for positive health promotion in the toddler group.

Adopt the habit of observing all child care personnel perform a return practice demonstration for diapers on a regular basis. Figures 4–3 and 4–4 provide an observation record to be used during the return practice procedure. In smaller program settings this could be practiced on a quarterly basis. In larger centers involving a broader range of staffing or one that is experiencing high turnover rates, employ return practice demonstrations once a month. The practice will keep everyone's diaper changing techniques sharp. It will also help shy personnel build their demonstration confidence for those occasional visits and observations conducted by the licensing agencies.

POTTY TRAINING

Most early care and education professionals and medical experts agree that one-year-olds are seldom ready to master the task of potty training. In past generations, parents were expected to have their children trained before two years of age. Parents are often pressured by older family members to conform to these outdated ideas, and this pressure often becomes the driving force behind initiating potty training before the toddler is ready. One-year-old children do begin to develop sphincter control for urine and bowel movement during this year. They will begin to experience longer periods of dryness. But for the most part during this age toddlers are very focused on a multitude of other areas of development and do not want to assume the responsibility of toilet training yet. In other words, their play time is a bigger priority to them than staying clean and dry. With that said, there is always an exception in every group and some particularly precocious toddler might begin to abhor wet diapers and will appreciate the opportunity to become toilet trained.

Return Practice Demonstration for Disposable Diapering Procedures

Name: _Erika_   Date: _7-13_

Observer: _Ms. Stevens_

Procedure:

_X_	Wash hands with liquid soap and water.
_X_	Gather supplies.
_X_	Put on disposable waterproof gloves (if used).
_X_	Cover diapering surface with nonabsorbent paper liner.
_X_	Place baby on prepared diaper area (minimize contact: hold baby away from your body if extremely wet or soiled).
_X_	Put soiled clothes in a plastic bag.
_X_	Unfasten diaper. Leave soiled diaper under the child.
_X_	Gently wash baby's bottom. Remove stool and urine from front to back, and use a fresh wipe each time. Dispose directly in designated receptacle.
_X_	Fold soiled diaper inward and place in designated receptacle followed by the disposable gloves (if used).
_X_	Use disposable wipe to clean surface of caregiver's hands and another to clean the child's.
_X_	Check for spills on paper. If present, fold over so fresh part is under buttocks.
_X_	Place clean diaper under baby.
_X_	Using a cotton ball or tissue, apply skin ointment to clean dry area if indicated/ordered.
_X_	Fasten diaper and dress with fresh clothing.
_X_	Wash baby's hands with soap and water between 60°F and 120°F for 15–20 seconds and dry. Turn faucet off with a paper towel, then place baby in a safe location.
_X_	Clean and disinfect diapering area, leaving bleach solution in contact at least 2 minutes. Allow table to air dry, or wipe it after 2 minutes.
_X_	Wash your hands with soap and water for at least 15–20 seconds. Turn off faucet with paper towel.
_X_	Chart diaper change and any observations.

FIGURE 4–3 Return Practice Demonstration for Disposable Diapering Procedures

Return Practice Demonstration for Cloth Diapering Procedures

Name: _Gregory_   Date: _7–13_

Observer: _Ms. Stanley_

Procedure:

_X_   Wash hands with liquid soap and water.

_X_   Gather supplies.

_X_   Put on disposable waterproof gloves (if used).

_X_   Cover diapering surface with nonabsorbent paper liner.

_X_   Place baby on prepared diaper area (minimize contact: hold baby away from your body if extremely wet or soiled).

_X_   Put soiled clothes in a plastic bag.

_X_   Unfasten diaper. Leave soiled diaper under the child. Close each safety pin immediately out of child's reach. Never hold pins in mouth.

_X_   Gently wash baby's bottom. Remove stool and urine from front to back, and use a fresh wipe each time. Dispose directly in designated receptacle.

_X_   Fold soiled diaper inward and place in designated receptacle followed by the disposable gloves (if used).

_X_   Use disposable wipe to clean surface of caregiver's hands and another to clean the child's.

_X_   Check for spills on paper. If present, fold over so fresh part is under buttocks.

_X_   Place clean diaper under baby.

_X_   Using a cotton ball or tissue, apply skin ointment to clean, dry area if indicated/ordered.

_X_   Fasten diaper with pins, placing your hand between the child and the diaper on insertion, and dress with fresh clothing.

_X_   Wash baby's hands with soap and water between 60°F and 120°F for 15–20 seconds and dry. Turn faucet off with a paper towel, then place baby in a safe location.

_X_   Clean and disinfect diapering area, leaving bleach solution in contact at least 2 minutes. Allow table to air dry, or wipe it after 2 minutes.

_X_   Wash your hands with soap and water for at least 15–20 seconds. Turn off faucet with paper towel.

_X_   Chart diaper change and any observations.

Figure 4–4 Return Practice Demonstration for Cloth Diapering Procedures

Set aside a time to discuss a plan with the toddler's family. This is a great topic to discuss at a one-year-old parenting class, parent teacher conference, or parent round table. The class will offer parents helpful information and provide active discussions. Advanced preparation increases the probability of more positive potty training experiences and in the long run saves the staff and the families time and frustration caused by unrealistic expectations for the toddler.

Toilet training is a collaborative effort that requires an open line of communication between home and the center. If at any time the toilet training is met with resistance, it bears slowing the process or stopping completely until the toddler has time to mature. Encourage parents to bring several changes of clothing, socks, training pants, and plastic pants covers. Choose clothing easy to remove or manage during "potty breaks." Disposable training pants that the toddler can pull up and down with ease are now available. Some programs and licensing agencies require the use of disposables to protect other children from harmful exposure brought on by an accident. They are well padded and will contain "accidents" during the course of training. Disposable training pants are the most expensive option, but most parents already use disposable diapers and feel the convenience makes them a reasonable choice. Sometimes the absorbent materials used in the disposable training pants mask the feeling of wetness and reduce the toddler's ability to distinguish between wet and dry.

An example of a typical Potty Training sheet used to record progress can be found in Figure 4–5. Review this sheet with the parents over the course of a few weeks to determine whether the toddler continues to demonstrate interest and is making progress. It is normal to expect a toddler to experience occasional accidents for the next few years.

Sometimes the toddler is very curious about initiating potty training, enthusiastically mimicking the procedure one moment, but then wants nothing to do with it the next. If at any time the child demonstrates resistance or cries when he or she is encouraged to sit on the potty chair, the child is most likely indicating the task is too much responsibility to assume at the moment. Discontinuing the program should be strongly considered.

STORING PERSONAL BELONGINGS/SANITATION STORAGE

If the parents are supplying diapers, request that they provide disposable diapers in unopened packages to ensure proper sanitation is maintained. Avoid storing the diapers on the floor. Store clothing, diapers, and personal items for each child in an individual container, cubby, or locker. Do not allow one child's personal belongings to touch another child's. This habit will reduce the potential cross-contamination of other children's personal items from germs or infestation, by contagious conditions such as head lice (pediculosis) or scabies, for instance.

HANDLING WET AND SOILED CLOTHING

When a child's clothing becomes wet or soiled, remove the soiled item and replace it with something clean and dry. Secure the soiled article of clothing in a plastic bag, and store it in a place for the parents to find at the time of departure. If the item is a soiled cloth diaper, secure it in a bag separate from the other articles of clothing. In order to ensure the clothing is not damaged or misplaced, do not launder any of the soiled clothing you take off of a toddler. Each parent has his or her own personal way of laundering clothing. To avoid mildewed clothing or permanent stains, send items home promptly. To prevent future misunderstandings when items are returned to parents, share this policy and its rationale with them at the time of enrollment.

POTTY TRAINING

Child's Name: _Grace_

Primary Caregiver: _Mrs. Carla_   **Date:** _June 3_

Time	Wet	B.M.	Dry	Refused	Seemed Confused	Comments
6:00 – 6:30						
6:30 – 7:00						
7:00 – 7:30						
7:30 – 8:00						Arrived
8:00 – 8:30	✓					
8:30 – 9:00			✓			
9:00 – 9:30			✓			
9:30 – 10:00			✓			
10:00 – 10:30	✓	✓				
10:30 – 11:00			✓			
11:00 – 11:30			✓			
11:30 – 12:00						Nap time diaper
12:00 – 12:30						
12:30 – 1:00						
1:00 – 1:30						
1:30 – 2:00						
2:00 – 2:30						Awake
2:30 – 3:00	✓					
3:00 – 3:30				✓		
3:30 – 4:00		✓				Accident, changed clothing
4:00 – 4:30						
4:30 – 5:00			✓			
5:00 – 5:30						Home at 5:10
5:30 – 6:00						
6:00 – 6:30						
6:30 – 7:00						
7:00 – 7:30						
7:30 – 8:00						

FIGURE 4–5 Potty Training Example

HAND WASHING PROCEDURES

Frequent hand washing is a cornerstone for a healthy early care and education program. Proper hand washing prevents the spread of many communicable diseases such as E. coli contamination (found largely in feces), hepatitis, giardia, pinworms, and a host of many more common ailments. All are spread through a fecal–oral route (anus to mouth).

Giardiasis and pinworms are the two most common parasitic infections among children in the United States. Wong (1999) found "the incidence of intestinal parasitic disease, especially giardiasis, has increased among young children who attend daycare centers" (p. 736). "Hand washing is the single most effective and critical measure and control of hepatitis in any setting" (p. 1577).

The best defense for reducing the spread of illness lies in consistent hand washing habits. The hand washing procedures shown in (Figure 4–6) are recommended for staff and children before and after playing in the sand and water table, after playing with pets, after playing outdoors, before and after preparing bottles or serving food, before and after diapering or toileting, before and after administering first aid, before and after giving medication, before working with children and at the end of the day, before leaving the classroom for a break, after wiping a nose, and after coughing or sneezing. Check with your local licensing agency for any other requirements in your area.

Install liquid soap with a pump or a dispenser and disposable paper towels near the sink. They are an integral part of hand washing. The National Center for Infectious Diseases (2005) encourages us to turn on the warm water (regulated by an antiscald device) and adjust it to achieve a comfortable temperature. Wet hands and apply liquid soap. Rub hands vigorously for approximately 15–20 seconds. The soap, along with the

Posted Hand Washing Procedures

1	Turn on warm water and adjust to comfortable temperature.	2	Wet hands and apply soap.	3	Wash vigorously for approximately 15–20 seconds.
4	Dry hands with paper towel.	5	Turn off faucet with paper towel.	6	Dispose of paper towel in a lidded trash receptacle with a plastic liner.

Use hand washing procedures for staff and children

- before and after preparing bottles or serving food.
- before and after diapering or toileting.
- before and after administering first aid.
- before and after giving medication.
- before working with the children and at the end of the day.
- before leaving the classroom for a break.
- after wiping nose discharge, coughing, or sneezing.
- before and after playing in the sand and water table.
- after playing with pets.
- after playing outdoors.

Reprinted with permission from the National Association of Child Care Professionals, http://www.naccp.org

FIGURE 4–6 Posted Hand Washing Procedures

scrubbing action, dislodges and removes germs. Rinse hands well and dry them with a clean paper towel. Be sure to wash under rings and the nails. Use a disposable paper towel to turn off the faucet and avoid recontaminating your clean hands. Dispose of the paper towel in a lidded trash receptacle with a plastic liner. A trash can operated with a foot mechanism is an expensive option, but the hands-free action reduces the possibility of recontaminating clean hands.

Install sinks with running hot (regulated by an antiscald device) and cold water, installed at the children's height to promote frequent use. Toddlers are able to move about the room quickly and they are fascinated with water found at a sink or in a toilet. Install an off-and-on water valve at the teachers' height to prevent curious toddlers from enjoying "unscheduled water play." Close bathroom doors when they are not in use, and do not leave buckets of water unattended to avoid a potential drowning.

Disinfect toilet seats, diapering areas, and water fountains with 10 percent bleach solution (one part chlorine bleach/nine parts water) or any registered EPA disinfectant prepared according to instructions. Registered EPA approval appears on the product label.

EMPLOYING UNIVERSAL PRECAUTIONS

In 1991 OSHA established a blood-borne pathogen standard mandating measures to protect employees from exposure to potentially infected blood pathogens. Hepatitis B (HBV) and Human Immunodeficiency Virus (HIV) are the two most common blood-borne pathogens. HBV is a disease of the liver contracted by exposure to contaminated blood. It causes inflammation and destruction of the liver and if not cured can eventually lead to death. HIV is a virus that is contracted by contaminated body fluids and has the potential to lead to AIDS, which destroys the human immune system.

Center staff are commonly exposed to body fluids in the form of urine, feces, vomitus, sweat, saliva, breast milk, and nasal secretions. It is difficult to stress the importance of using universal precautions without sounding a fear alarm. Contracting a case of HIV/AIDS is highly unlikely; in fact, Kinnell reports "the Centers for Disease Control and Prevention stated 'we have never documented a case of HIV being transmitted through biting.' Because it is impossible to know when a person is infected with such a disease *all* body fluids or secretions *must* be treated as if they are infected with disease" (p. 54).

In the event that exposure to another person's body fluids is necessary, put on a pair of disposable, moisture-proof gloves before making contact with the contaminated source. To avoid delaying immediate intervention on behalf of the child, yet protect yourself from harmful exposure, place gloves in several convenient areas so they can be retrieved quickly. To avoid contaminating yourself with soiled gloves, take care to remove them properly. Instructions for proper gloving procedures are located in Appendix C. Post this next to the first aid directives for a quick reference. Follow your company's policies for disposal of contaminated supplies and equipment.

DENTAL HYGIENE

The Centers for Disease Control and Prevention offer several recommendations for tooth care for young children. It is recommended that teeth be cleaned early using a small, soft toothbrush. Toddlers are not capable of holding a brush and will require assistance. Until they are two years of age, avoid fluoride toothpastes unless their dentist recommends it. Only use a small pea-size amount of toothpaste. Teach them to rinse and spit out the toothpaste after brushing. The toothbrushes will need to be stored in individual containers labeled with each child's name. In some states the toothbrushes are to be stored so they can air-dry. To avoid cross-contamination, the toothbrushes should not touch. Discard and replace the toothbrushes each time a child experiences a serious cold, flu, fever, or other communicable disease in order to avoid a cycle of recontamination. Children need to brush their teeth at least twice a day. Involve the parents when planning a schedule. It might be most feasible to have toddlers brush their teeth in the morning before they come to the center and in the evening after their family dinner. The center staff could promote positive oral care habits by providing water for the little ones to rinse their mouths after eating. See the end of the chapter for the Center for Disease Control and Prevention Web site to find helpful information to share with the toddler's family to promote positive dental hygiene habits.

CLEANSING TOYS AND EQUIPMENT

A toddler will place toys in his or her mouth. Because you are providing care for a group of toddlers, it is important to maintain proper sanitation of the toys and the equipment they use each day. Provide a container such as a bucket or basket labeled "soiled toys" (see Figure 4–7). After a toddler has finished playing with a toy, place it in the bucket or basket. At convenient times throughout the day, cleanse the toys with a sanitizing solution such as a bleach solution of 50 parts per million (approximately ½ teaspoon of chlorine bleach to 1 gallon of water). Once the toys have completely dried they are ready for use again. Use this same preparation to sanitize high chairs, cribs, tables, and chairs between uses by different children.

Soiled Toys

FIGURE 4–7 Labeled Soiled Toys Container

REFERENCES

American Academy of Pediatrics, American Public Health Association, National Resource Center for Health and Safety in Child Care. (2002). *Stepping stones to using caring for our children* (2nd ed.). Elk Grove, IL: American Academy of Pediatrics.

Centers for Disease Control and Prevention. (2005). *Brush up on healthy teeth: Simple steps for kids' smiles.* Retrieved March 8, 2005, from http://www.cdc.gov

Indiana State Board of Health. (2002). *Sanitizing solutions.* Retrieved January 1, 2005, from http://www.in.gov/icpr/webfile/formsdiv/46684.pdf.

Kinnell, G. (2002). *No biting.* St. Paul, MN: Red Leaf Press.

National Association of Child Care Professionals and National Accreditation Commission. (2005). *Washing hands.* Retrieved April 15, 2005, from http://www.naccp.org

National Center for Infectious Diseases. (2005). *An ounce of prevention keeps the germs away.* Retrieved March 8, 2005, from http://www.cdc.gov/ncidod/op/handwashing.htm

Wong, D. (1999). *Whaley & Wong's care of infants and children.* St. Louis, MO: Mosby.

RECOMMENDED RESOURCES

California Department of Education. (1995). *Keeping kids healthy: Preventing and managing communicable disease in child care.* Sacramento, CA.

Church, D. S. (2004). *The MELALEUCA wellness guide* (8th ed.). Littleton, CO: RM Barry Publications.

Donowitz, L. G. (2002). *Infection control in the child care center and preschool.* (6th ed.). Portland: Williams & Wilkins.

Indiana State Board of Health. (2000). *Supplemental health program for child care centers providing infant–toddler care hand washing procedure.* http://www.in.gov

Reisser, P. C. (1997). *Baby & child care.* Carol Stream, IL: Tyndale House.

To find your specific
State's Licensing, Rules
and Regulations go to:

http://nrc.uchsc.edu

CHAPTER

5

Health

SICK BAY AND ISOLATION AREA

Centers need to prepare a sick bay and an isolation area for a sick child to rest until a parent or guardian can call for him or her. Equip a space or room (depending on state regulations) with a bed or cot and a crib in an area where a child can be supervised constantly. Sometimes space is very limited and a cot in the director's office will have to suffice. If a bed is used, provide several changes of linens so each child uses a new set. Select a variety of toys and books to offer the little one until his or her departure. Provide a thermometer to measure body temperature and a container large enough to catch emesis in case the child vomits. Place a child-size chair in the area for a child to sit in while you administer first aid. For convenience, locate a locked medication/first aid cabinet and a small refrigerator nearby stocked with a lidded container labeled "refrigerated medications only," ice in baggies or cold packs, popsicles (for mouth and lip injuries), juice boxes, and fresh drinking water.

FIRST AID CABINET AND FIRST AID KITS

Minor injuries are common in a center setting. Children will experience scratches and bumps as they go about their daily activities. Prepare a first aid cabinet and kits to use in the event of an accident. As previously mentioned, it is convenient to provide a first aid cabinet near the area used to isolate sick children. The first aid cabinet must remain locked at all times so it is not accessible to the children but is accessible to the staff at a moment's notice. If your center transports children, then provide a complete first aid kit in the vehicle. Stock the first aid cabinet with disposable nonporous gloves and an American Red Cross first aid manual, American Academy of Pediatrics (AAP) standard first aid chart, or an equivalent first aid guide. Other items to include are a nonglass thermometer, bandages, Band-Aids, sterile gauze pads, a triangular cloth splint, a plastic splint for immobilizing a limb, scissors, tweezers, safety pins, adhesive strips, a disposable apron, protective glasses, and a pocket mouth-to-mouth resuscitation mask to open an airway.

Causing vomiting when a caustic or corrosive substance has been swallowed can cause further physical damage; for this reason best practices no longer recommends the use of syrup of ipecac in child care facilities.

Provide a source for running water and soap near the first aid station to cleanse wounds. If running water is not available on a field trip, use a waterless antiseptic hand cleaner. All items contaminated with blood should be placed in plastic bags. These materials must be handled according to your center policy.

First aid supplies should also be conveniently available on the playground. Some centers find it convenient to hang a fanny pack in each classroom near the door so the teacher can wear it on the playground or use it in the classroom for minor injuries. Because accidents on the playground often involve blood, the teacher will need to employ universal

Daily Medication Sheet

Child's Name	RX Number & Type of Medication	Amount & Route Administered	Date	Time	Given By:	
					First Name	Last Name
Carmela (Enter last name)	RX 652201 Amoxicillin 250 Milligrams	1 tsp by mouth	02-22	11:00 am	Mrs.	Hoffriah
				5:00 pm	Mrs.	Szalay

FIGURE 5–1 Daily Medication Sheet

precautions before handling the hurt child. If a fanny pack is not used, another option on the playground involves installing a mailbox on a post. Stock the mailbox with items such as disposable nonporous gloves, tissues, wipes, plastic trash bags, sterile gauze pads, and Band-Aids. The mailbox will keep the items dry until they are needed.

ADMINISTERING AND MANAGING MEDICATIONS

Administering medications requires special attention to detail. In some states all personnel distributing medication must take a special class and earn a certification. Check your local regulations. Instruct all personnel to always wash their hands before administering medication and to make sure they always match the name of the child with the label on the medication. Double-check the proper dose. Always use a medication spoon or measuring spoon to be certain the proper dosage is administered. Follow the instructions for how frequently it should be given and whether it should be given before or after eating. Once the medication is given, document it on the Daily Medication Sheet shown in Figure 5–1. The directions for using the Daily Medication sheet are explained further in this chapter.

Medications prescribed for an individual child should be kept in the original container bearing the original pharmacy label showing the prescription number, the date it was filled, the physician's name, directions for use, and the child's name. Send medication home every day with the child. If the child requires a repeat dosage the following day, begin with fresh instructions and do not rely on information from the preceding day. For the protection of the child and yourself, do not give any over-the-counter medications without prior written approval from the child's physician and the child's parents. Written permission from the parents and the child's physician is a standard most states require. Check with your licensing consultant.

Occasionally a child will develop symptoms of illness, such as a high fever, persistent cough, or ear pain caused by an infection. Although most programs are not equipped to provide continuous sick care, there often is a lapse in time before the parents/guardians can arrive to attend to their ill child. It takes time to locate working parents, especially if they are not in the office or if they must wait for a replacement before leaving work (e.g., nurses or firefighters). Have presigned, approved physician orders on hand for fever-reducing medications and such. Use the Medical Authorization for Nonprescription Medications form shown in Figure 5–2. Give medications only with this preapproved authorization and under the written direction of the parents at the beginning of the shift. Use the Daily Medication sheet to document the administration of medications throughout the day. It includes the date; the child's name; the type of medication; the dosage; and the route of administration such as by mouth or in the eyes, ears, or rectum; and how often the dosage should be repeated. Sign the record with your full name and the time the medication is administered to maintain an accurate medication history. Store all medications requiring refrigeration in a container with a secure lid labeled *refrigerated medications only*. Store any medications that do not require refrigeration in a locked cabinet that is inaccessible to the children. Figure 5–3 provides instructions for creating a file box to store the current copies of Medical Authorization for Nonprescription Medications sheets. Since you will need to refer to the permission slips quite frequently, it is helpful to store them in an easily accessible location such as in or near the locked medicine cabinet. Place the Daily Medication record on a clipboard near the Beginning the Day clipboard discussed in Chapter 7, "Facilitating Toddlers and Their Families." Place the clipboard at the entrance to your room or facility to make it easy for the parents or guardians to record daily medication instructions.

Many medications are required to be given every 4–6 hours, or on a schedule of three times a day or four times a day. Most antibiotics can now be prescribed twice a day or every 10–12 hours. Consider creating a schedule to administer the majority of medications at specific times. Specifying what times medications are usually administered guides the parents to pick a schedule that is convenient for the center and simultaneously adheres to the proper dosage regimen for the specific medication. Encourage the parents to administer the first dose in the morning before the child arrives at the center. Mornings typically are very busy and the center staff is occupied with so many details, a medication dosage could easily be missed. Especially during the winter months it is common for the number of children on medications to increase substantially. Suggest that the center be responsible for the midday dose administered typically around lunchtime and another around 4:00 or 5:00 pm, leaving the evening dose for the parents to administer (adjusting the times, of course, if you are open nontraditional hours). There will always be occasional exceptions to the scheduled times, such as a sudden need for an asthma treatment. Scheduling the majority of the medications to be given at the same time will decrease the risk of missing treatments and doses and increase the accuracy of administration.

On a final note, if your program also serves infants, for a myriad of reasons, infant medication schedules are better served by providing the infant room a separate Daily Medication record. For one, infants' on-demand schedule for eating and sleeping is quite different from that of the other age groups. Unless you have a very small number of children in your program, separate the infants' Daily Medication record from the toddler through school age Daily Medication record.

Medical Authorization
for Nonprescription Medication *

Name of Child: _____Jessie (Enter Last Name)_____   Date: _____09-18-2009_____

The staff is authorized to dispense the following medications as ordered by your physician and directed by the parents/guardians.

Please indicate specific medication, route it is to be given, dosage, and frequency.

Type	Medication	Route	Dosage	Frequency
Nonaspirin Preparation	Tylenol	By mouth	.4 cc	Every 4 hours over 101° as needed Send Home
Aspirin Preparation				
Cough Preparation	Robitussin	By mouth	1/2 tsp	Every 6 hours for persistent cough
Decongestant				
Skin Ointment	Desitin	On perineum	Thin layer	Every diaper change when redness develops
Diaper Wipes	Any brand	As directed		As needed
Sunscreen	Any brand	On skin	Small amount	Before outdoor play

_____Dr. Randall_____   _____Dr. Randall_____   _____xxx-xxx-xxxx_____
Print Name of Physician   Signature of Physician   Phone Number

_____Collin (Enter Last Name)_____
Parent/Guardian Signature

* Complete this form on admission and update annually. Store medical authorizations in an index box and place in or near locked cabinet for quick referencing.

FIGURE 5–2 Medical Authorization Form

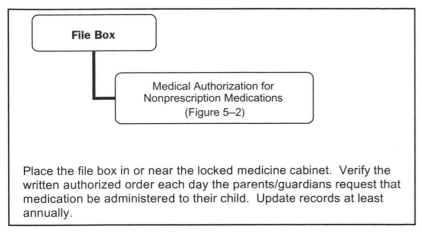

FIGURE 5–3 File Box for Record Keeping

MEASURING BODY TEMPERATURE

If you suspect a child is overly warm or has an elevated temperature, measure and record his or her body temperature. The safest way to record a child's temperature is under the arm, also known as an axillary temperature. The average normal axillary temperature is 97.4°F, or 36.3°C. If you are using a plastic (nonglass) thermometer, be sure to shake the mercury reading below 98°F before measuring the child's temperature. Hold the thermometer under the child's arm for 10 minutes. Mercury is extremely toxic and can cause a hazard if the thermometer is broken and it escapes. If that ever occurs, call Poison Control to receive specific instructions. For convenience, many centers opt to use more expensive thermometer strips for the forehead or electronic thermometers. If you use an electronic thermometer, then hold it in place until you hear a beeping sound.

Report an elevated body temperature immediately. Initiate an illness report and notify the attending supervisor so the parents/guardians can be contacted. Medicate the child if instructed by the parents/guardians or physician. Record the child's temperature reading on a Suggested Illness record (Figure 5–4). Continue checking the temperature every 30 minutes to monitor any changes. A child who has experienced an elevated temperature should not return to the group until his or her temperature has been normal for 24 hours unless advised differently by a physician.

ALLERGIES AND POSTING ALLERGY NOTICES

Allergies are caused by a variety of culprits known as allergens. Some can be triggered by a range of substances that include: venom, nuts, latex, certain drugs, stings, pollen, dust, mold, animal dander, and shellfish. A severe reaction can occur quickly, usually within a few minutes. Severe reactions are usually dramatic, with symptoms such as swelling of the face; tight, difficult breathing; or hives that look like red blotches on the skin. Mild allergic reactions are more common than severe ones. Milder allergic reactions display the same symptoms in much weaker forms and take longer to develop. Local reactions such as swelling of an entire arm or leg can be severe but are not commonly lethal. If a child has a severe allergy, recommend that the child wear a Medic Alert bracelet for immediate identification of the allergen if an exposure ever occurs. Severe reactions can be life threatening. Anaphylactic shock will very quickly interfere with the child's ability to breathe. If a child in attendance at the center has a known anaphylactic shock history, then a kit for epinephrine injections

SUGGESTED ILLNESS

Child's name: _Steven (Enter Last Name)_   Date: _____1/13_____

SYMPTOMS ARE:

___101.1___   Body Temperature (under arm, add 1 degree)

____x____   Vomiting

_____   Diarrhea

_____   Exhibiting signs of a communicable illness

_____   Skin condition requiring further treatment

Other: _____lethargic, listless_____

Report initiated by: _____D.O._____

Were parents notified? Yes __x__ No _____ By whom? ___D.O.___

Time parents notified: 1st Attempt _10:45_   ___Mom___
                                                        Which Parent Notified
                           2nd Attempt _11:00_   ___Mom___
                                                        Which Parent Notified
                           3rd Attempt _____   _____
                                                        Which Parent Notified

Time child departed: _12:15_

Director's signature: _____Ms. Marshall_____

Children exhibiting a temperature that exceeds 100°F, symptoms of vomiting (1–3 forceful rushes), diarrhea (defined as watery, mucous, foul-smelling bowel movement), or an unrecognized rash shall not return to group care for a minimum of 24 hours after treatment or before symptoms subside.

1. Office Copy   2. Parent/Guardian Copy

Figure 5–4 Suggested Illness

should remain on the premises and all staff should be familiar with how to administer it. Call 9-1-1 or the appropriate number if the toddler is exposed to a known allergen or begins to exhibit signs of a severe reaction. Milder reactions, although not life threatening, will need a doctor's care, especially if the reaction has not occurred before.

On the *KIDEX for Ones* Individual Monthly Profile and Introduce Us to Your Toddler, a space is provided for listing and recording any allergies a child might have. Always post a list of all children and their known allergies in the KIDEX Class Book.

ILLNESS RECORDS AND TRACKING ILLNESS REPORTS

Begin each day with a general health assessment of each child. Familiarity with each child will help you to become a reliable detector of unusual physical symptoms. If a child has a preexisting medical condition or a physical disability, become familiar with his or her particular needs.

Minor illnesses are often indicated by a change in a child's general appearance or behavior, such as glassy eyes, flushed cheeks, swollen glands, or sluggish movements. Isolate sick children from the group if they have a temperature that exceeds 100°F, symptoms of vomiting (one to three forceful rushes), diarrhea (defined as a watery, mucous, foul-smelling bowel movement), or an undiagnosed rash. If you suspect a child is exhibiting any of these symptoms, then complete an illness report with details and give it to the director to initiate the next step. Once the director confirms the child is sick, then notify the parents.

Parents often feel frustration and guilt coupled with anxiety about having a sick child and missing work. Be certain the child is ill before disturbing the parents. If at any time a child is exposed to a communicable illness such as chicken pox, measles, and so on, then post a notice on the Current Events Bulletin Board. Descriptions of common communicable illnesses and symptoms can be found in Chapter 8 and in other books in the KIDEX series for children under the age of five.

A local pediatrician mentioned once how much she appreciated written documentation accompanying a sick child who had just arrived from a center. She indicated that all too often parents bring a child to be examined with little or no information regarding the symptoms the child has been experiencing. Provide the parents with a copy of the Suggested Illness report to take with them to the physician so they will have details in hand about the symptoms. Track reports of illnesses on a daily basis to help identify potential outbreak patterns that might be developing in the center (see Figure 5–5).

HOW TO PREVENT A HEAD LICE INFESTATION

Whenever children are cared for in groups, head lice infestation is possible. Children with head lice usually have older siblings who attend elementary school and unsuspectingly carry it home to their family. Head lice are a potential problem but do not indicate a family is dirty; it can happen to anyone. Head lice can be picked up anywhere, such as in movie theaters, on a bus, or from an airline seat. In a child care setting the problem is more likely to occur if infested clothing touches other clothing.

To reduce the possibility of a head lice epidemic in your center, the program will need to be proactive and employ weekly head checks for every child. Figure 5–6 includes an example of a completed Head Lice Checklist. Take measures to ensure this information remains confidential. Head checks need to occur on a different day each week to include all children attending, especially those with a part-time schedule. Plan to administer head

Illness Tracking Reports

Name of Child	Date	Time Called	Type of Illness	Person Reporting Illness	Director Notified	Report Filed	Parent Notified	Time Left
Emily (Enter Last Name)	1/26	12:30 pm	Fever 101°	Mrs. Willis	✓	✓	✓	1:30 pm
Jaden (Enter Last Name)	1/27	11:00 am	Diarrhea	Ms. Sutton	✓	✓	✓	11:15 am
Olivia (Enter Last Name)	1/27	2:00 pm	Vomiting	Mr. Thurmond	✓	✓	✓	2:30 pm
Marta (Enter Last Name)	1/28	7:30 am	Ear Ache	Mrs. Hiland	✓	✓	✓	8:00 am
Chen (Enter Last Name)	1/29	8:15 am	Headache	Mrs. Day	✓	✓	✓	8:45 am
Joshua (Enter Last Name)	1/30	4:00 pm	Split Lip	Mr. Law	✓	✓	✓	4:30 pm
Andrew (Enter Last Name)	1/30	4:30 pm	Fever 100°	Ms. Lane	✓	✓	✓	4:45 pm

FIGURE 5–5 Illness Tracking Reports

checks right after a nap period when children are having their hair brushed and combed. Make sure you are in a well-lit area. You might see a louse, but they move very quickly and you might only detect their eggs (nits). As you comb the hair, observe the hair roots for any little nits. They often attach about ¼–½ inch from the hair root. They are very tiny and translucent. It is easy to distinguish between a nit and a skin flake. A nit will not move very easily since it is more firmly attached than a skin flake.

A head louse does not live very long without a warm-blooded host, in this case human beings. In order for head lice to survive, they must obtain nutrition from their host. Head lice infestation can be treated by using special shampoos formulated to destroy the live lice and their eggs. Check with your local pharmacist for other recommendations. Send all personal (belongs to family) bedding home with the families to be laundered in hot water.

If you discover a child with a potential problem, contact his or her parents immediately and isolate the child from other children until he or she departs. Send home all of the child's blankets, soft toys, pillows, hats, and coats, as well as any other personal items that might harbor head lice or their eggs. Instruct the families to launder all washable items in hot water and dry them on high heat for at least 20 minutes. Nonwashable items can be bagged in plastic trash bags and left for a week or so before being used again. Sprays are available to kill lice and nits on items if a quicker turnaround is needed, such as for a favorite stuffed bunny. Do not allow the infested child to return to the program until all evidence of nits has been removed from his or her hair. To prevent the spread of head lice and reduce the possibility of an epidemic, check every child's head for five days past the last discovery.

Head Lice Checklist

Group Name: _____The Peaches_____

Name	Sunday	Monday	Tuesday	Wednesday	Thursday	Friday	Saturday
		April 29	May 7	May 15	May 23	May 31	
Bailey (Enter last name)		A	C	C	A	A	
Emily (Enter last name)		C	C	C	C	C	
Jared (Enter last name)		C	C	C	C	C	
Jenni (Enter last name)		C	C	A	C	C	
Mary (Enter last name)		C	C	C	C	C	
Robert (Enter last name)		C	C	C	C	C	
Kellie (Enter last name)		C	A	C	C	C	
Erin (Enter last name)		C	C	C	C	C	

C = Clear   A = Absent   P = Possible

(**Reminder:** Please check weekly on different days of the week.)

FIGURE 5–6 Head Lice Checklist

Cross-contamination can be a challenge if measures are not employed to separate personal items such as combs and brushes. It is tempting to discourage children from bringing combs and brushes to the center. Yet positive opportunities to interact with each child during grooming far outweigh the measures required to reduce such occurrences. The children need to be touched in positive ways during the day, and hair brushing and combing are a wonderful way to do this. Separate and store hair items in individual closed containers. Resealable plastic bags available at the grocery store are inexpensive and work very well. Label each storage container, comb, and brush with the child's name.

A diligent effort to maintain stringent hygienic practices and regular head checks will thwart the possibility of an epidemic in your program.

RECOMMENDED RESOURCES

Aronson, S. S., & Shope, T. R. *Managing infectious diseases in child care and schools.* Elk Grove Village, IL: American Academy of Pediatrics.

Kemper, K. J. (1996). *The holistic pediatrician.* New York: HarperCollins.

HELPFUL WEB SITES

Health and Safety Tips, *Immunizations.* http://nrc.uchsc.edu

Health and Safety Tips, *Medication administration in the child care setting.* http://nrc.uchsc.edu

Health and Safety Tips, *Daily health checks.* http://nrc.uchsc.edu

PLACES TO PURCHASE FIRST AID SUPPLIES

Child Care Workers Compliance Guidelines for
the OSHA Blood-Borne Pathogen Standard

Professional Medical Enterprises

450 Bedford Street

Lexington, MA 02173

Coney Safety Products

1-800-356-9100

http://www.coney.com

Video for Blood-Borne Pathogens

Coastal Training Company

3083 Brickhouse Court

Virginia Beach, VA 23452

Fax: 804-498-3657

Info:1-800-767-7703

http://www. coastal.com

To find your specific
State's Licensing, Rules
and Regulations go to:

http://nrc.uchsc.edu

CHAPTER

6

Safety

POSTING FIRST AID DIRECTIVES

Early care and education professionals who are adequately trained in cardiopulmonary resuscitation (CPR), artificial respiration, and first aid procedures are an asset to the children they care for. It is advisable for all child care personnel to receive and maintain current CPR, artificial respiration, and first aid training.

Post first aid directives in each room to serve as a quick reminder of what steps to follow in case of an emergency. First aid directives are a brief review of what to do if an emergency does occur. There are many different kinds of emergencies. In Figure 6–1 some of the most common emergencies are listed, such as: poisoning, bleeding, choking, seizures, shock, and situations requiring artificial respiration. Place the directives next to each phone along with the phone numbers for the poison control center, the fire department, emergency help, medical, dental, ambulance, and the police station. When pertinent information is readily available in an emergency situation, it can help staff remain calm enough to perform at an optimum level.

LEAVING THE ROOM UNATTENDED

Child/adult ratios are established and maintained for classroom safety. A room with children present should *never* be left unattended by an adult! Leaving children unattended puts them in a potentially dangerous situation. Open your door and alert someone, or pick up the telephone (if it's nearby) and page for help. When it becomes necessary to leave your room, arrange for another adult to cover for you.

SAFETY AND ACCIDENT PREVENTION

SAFE USA (2002) reports that in one year, approximately "7,000 children were sent to the hospital for falls from high chairs." Always employ the use of the safety strap the moment the toddler is placed in most equipment such as high chairs or strollers. The most effective straps include a waist strap and one that extends between the legs. The latter strap prevents the baby from slipping down in a seat and being strangled. The safety straps in your center will sustain heavy usage and eventually wear thin and require replacement long before the equipment has served its full life. The straps can be replaced by the original manufacturer or found from a source such as Custom Straps, http://www.ahh.biz or toll free 1-866-458-2559.

Some accidents are caused by a high chair tipping over. A high chair might tip if an active child pushes off from a table or wall, stands up in the high chair, or rocks back and forth. Pick high chairs that have wide bases.

SUGGESTED FIRST AID DIRECTIVES

CHOKING

(Conscious) - Stand or kneel behind child with your arms around his waist and make a fist. Place thumb side of fist in the middle of abdomen just above the navel. With moderate pressure, use your other hand to press fist into child's abdomen with a quick, upward thrust. Keep your elbows out and away from child. Repeat thrusts until obstruction is cleared or child begins to cough or becomes unconscious.

(Unconscious) - Position child on his back. Just above navel, place heel of one hand on the midline of abdomen with the other hand placed on top of the first. Using moderate pressure, press into abdomen with a quick, upward thrust. Open airway by tilting head back and lifting chin. **If you can see the object**, do a finger sweep. Slide finger down inside of cheek to base of tongue, sweep object out but be careful not to push the object deeper into the throat. Repeat above until obstruction is removed or child begins coughing. If child does not resume breathing, proceed with artificial respiration (see below).

Infants - Support infant's head and neck. Turn infant face down on your forearm. Lower your forearm onto your thigh. Give four (4) back blows forcefully between infant's shoulder blades with heel of hand. Turn infant onto back. Place middle and index fingers on breastbone between nipple line and end of breastbone. Quickly compress breastbone one-half to one inch with each thrust. Repeat backblows and chest thrusts until object is coughed up, infant starts to cry, cough, and breathe, or medical personnel arrives and takes over.

POISONING

Call Poison Control Center (1-800-382-9097) immediately! Have the poison container handy for reference when talking to the center. Do not induce vomiting unless instructed to do so by a health professional. Check the child's airway, breathing, and circulation.

HEMORRHAGING

Use a protective barrier between you and the child (gloves). Then, with a clean pad, apply firm continuous pressure to the bleeding site for five minutes. Do not move/change pads, but you may place additional pads on top of the original one. If bleeding persists, call the doctor or ambulance Open wounds may require a tetanus shot.

SEIZURE

Clear the area around the child of hard or sharp objects. Loosen tight clothing around the neck. Do not restrain the child. Do not force fingers or objects into the child's mouth. After the seizure is over and if the child is not experiencing breathing difficulties, lay him/her on his/her side until he/she regains consciousness or until he/she can be seen by emergency medical personnel. After the seizure, allow the child to rest. Notify parents immediately. If child is experiencing breathing difficulty, or if seizure is lasting longer than 15 minutes, call an ambulance at once.

ARTIFICIAL RESPIRATION *(Rescue Breathing)*

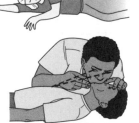

Position child on the back; if not breathing, open airway by gently tilting the head back and lifting chin. Look, listen, and feel for breathing. If still not breathing, keep head tilted back and pinch nose shut. Give two full breaths and then one regular breath every 4 seconds thereafter. Continue for one minute; then look, listen, and feel for the return of breathing. Continue rescue breathing until medical help arrives or breathing resumes.

If using one-way pulmonary resuscitation device, be sure your mouth and child's mouth are sealed around the device.

(Modification for infants only)   Proceed as above, but place your mouth over nose and mouth of the infant. Give light puffs every 3 seconds.

SHOCK

If skin is cold and clammy, as well as face pale or child has nausea or vomiting, or shallow breathing, call for emergency help. Keep the child lying down. Elevate the feet. If there are head/chest injuries, raise the head and shoulders only.

Figure 6–1 Suggest First Aid Directives

Safety Plug Covers

For the safety of all the children, check electrical outlets for safety plug covers on a daily basis. *It is important for safety covers to be in place at all times.* Toddlers are curious, and an unprotected electrical outlet offers the potential for electrocution. Standard 5.048, Safety Covers and Shock Protection Devices for Electrical Outlets, Caring for Our Children, National Health and Safety Performance Standards (2nd ed.), encourages the use of safety plug covers that are attached to the electrical receptacle by a screw or other means to prevent easy removal by a child. Avoid using outlet covers that a child can pull from the socket. All newly installed electrical outlets accessible to children should be protected by GFCI shock protection devices or safety receptacles that require simultaneous contact with both prongs of a plug to access the electricity (American Academy of Pediatrics 2002). Several new safety plug outlets are now available for consumers. If you are planning new construction, consider placing the electrical outlets at least 48 inches from the ground.

Latex Balloons and Small Object Hazards

Latex balloons can be a very dangerous toy for infants and young children. Because they explore with their mouths, it is not uncommon for a baby or toddler to suck or bite a balloon, causing it to burst. Preschool children may attempt to inflate a balloon and run the risk of it deflating and blocking their airway. Best practices strongly discourage latex balloons, and they should not be permitted in a child care facility where young children are present. If the center shares playground space with school-age children, be very careful to clean up any latex pieces left by the older children. The same advice holds for toy lending and swapping. For instance, if an older class borrows a set of the younger group's building blocks to help construct a "block city," double-check the returned items for any errant small objects such as marbles or puzzle pieces that could present a hazard for the younger group.

Crib and Mattress Safety

If you are using cribs with adjustable mattress heights, lower the mattress as appropriate to match the growth of the toddler in order to avoid a dangerous fall. Many cribs have a bed rail that moves up and down. Avoid a head injury or dangerous fall by placing the crib rail up and in a locked position at all times when a child is occupying the bed.

Choose sturdy cribs with bars that are not more 2⅜ inches apart. Many companies offer heavy-duty portacrib-size beds. A firm waterproof mattress is your best choice. The gap between the mattress and the crib should not exceed 1 inch to prevent possible suffocation.

The bed is not an appropriate place for extended play. Once a toddler awakens from his or her nap, remove him or her promptly to a more appropriate play area.

INDIVIDUAL ACCIDENT REPORT AND ACCIDENT TRACKING REPORT

If a child is injured during the course of the day, complete an Accident/Incident Report (see Figure 6–2). The report will describe the type of injury, its location on the body, and what time it occurred. It will also answer the following questions: Was blood present? If so, were universal precautions employed? What type of treatment was rendered, and who witnessed the accident? After this report is completed, send it to the director for review. Contact the family and inform them of the injuries so they can decide, with the center personnel, if they desire further treatment for their child. Some parents are more likely to seek medical treatment than others, and it is a decision they are entitled to make. *Some states require the center/teacher to submit a copy of the accident report to their licensing consultant if the injury required medical intervention by a doctor, clinic, or hospital.* This form is a legal document so great care must be exercised to complete it accurately. Describe the injury rather than assign a diagnosis. For example, describe an injury as a purple mark the size of a dime on the right cheek rather than a bruise or contusion on the face. If you are unsure of how to describe an injury accurately, it is best to obtain assistance from a supervisor.

In large child care centers it is helpful to track trends regarding illness or accidents. Create a binder specifically to collect and record all accident and illness reports. On a daily basis, log accidents and illnesses using the Accident/Incident Tracking Report (see Figure 6–3). This will require only a few moments. The director can use it as a handy reference to track possible illness trends such as influenza or RSV or perhaps discover a pattern of accidents occurring in a specific group, such as biting or falls. If your center maintains a copy of individual Accident/Incident Reports or Suggested Illness reports, discussed in Chapter 5, "Health," store them in the binder with the Accident/Incident Tracking Reports so they do not become part of the child's permanent record. Figure 6–4 provides guidance for creating a binder to house emergency and safety information. It is not uncommon for government agencies such as the Occupational Safety and Health Administration (OSHA), local fire marshals, firefighting personnel, or staff from program licensing agencies to visit and request to see this type of information.

POSTING EMERGENCY EVACUATION PLANS AND EMERGENCY PHONE NUMBER LISTS

Place by every phone a list of emergency contacts for quick reference (see Figure 6–5). Conduct emergency drills at least monthly. Every room where children are cared for requires a very specific outline of instructions and procedures that are to be followed in case of an emergency. Post this in a visible location. The instructions need to include what exit to use in a situation requiring the children to be removed from the building (see Figures 6–6 and 6–7).

When it is necessary to remove the toddlers from the building, place them in a sturdy bed that has been prepared with heavy wheel casters and follow the specific instructions outlined for the emergency exit procedure.

CONDUCTING EMERGENCY EVACUATION DRILLS

Familiarize yourself with evacuation information long before a drill occurs. It is helpful to have a large blanket and an emergency bag available in case re-entry to the building is delayed (see Figure 6–8 for how to assemble an emergency bag). Maintain a replenished emergency bag at all times so it is available at a moment's notice. Schedule drills to be conducted on a regular basis. Toddlers are often afraid of the loud sound of an alarm. Talk to them and prepare them for the drill ahead of time.

RECORDING EMERGENCY EVACUATION DRILLS

Keep a record of what day and time emergency drills take place, as well as how long it takes for the center to completely evacuate all the children *safely* to their designated areas. Evacuation drill examples are provided for hurricanes (Figure 6–9), tornadoes (Figure 6–10), and earthquakes (Figure 6–11). Figures 6–12 and 6–13 provide examples of the Tornado/Earthquake Drill Log and Building Evacuation Log. Customize the templates provided in the Forms and Templates Appendix for your center.

Accident/Incident

Child's Name: _____ John (Enter Last Name) _____

Date of accident/injury: _____ 6/1 _____ Time: _____ 3:00 _____

Brief description of accident/injury: _____ John tripped and hit his head on the edge of a table. _____

Was first aid given? _____ yes _____ If so, describe: _____ Ms. Callhoon pressed a cold pack against the small bump. _____

Was blood present in accident? _____ no _____ How much? _____

Were Universal Precautions employed? _____

Was medical intervention required?* _____ no _____ If yes, describe: _____

Person initiating this report: _____ Ms. Smith _____ Witness: _____ Ms. Johnson _____

Name of parent contacted: Emily (Enter Last Name) Time contacted: _____ 3:15 _____

Director's signature: _____ Ms. Smith _____

* In some states it is required to file a copy of this report with the child care licensing department if medical intervention is required.

FIGURE 6–2 Accident/Incident Report

Accident/Incident Tracking Reports

Name of Child	Date	Time Called	Type of Accident	Person Reporting Accident	Director Notified	Report Filed	Parent Notified	Time Left
Elijah (Enter Last Name)	9/1	9:00	Fell off tricycle, no injury noted	Ms. Marsh	Yes	Yes	Yes	9:10
Hailey (Enter Last Name)	9/1	11:30	Paper cut	Ms. Smith	Yes	Yes	Yes	11:45
Shakarri (Enter Last Name)	9/1	3:45	Tripped on edge of mat, bit lip slightly	Ms. Marsh	Yes	Yes	Yes	4:00

Figure 6–3 Accident/Incident Tracking Report

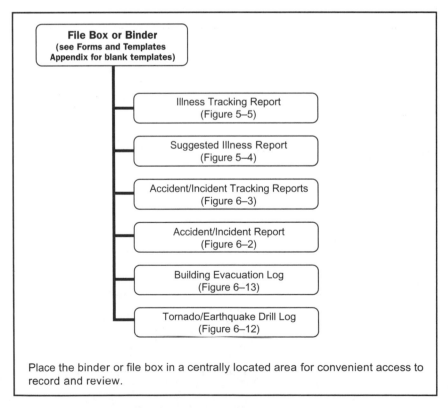

Figure 6–4 File Box for Record Keeping

Emergency Contacts: *Post Near Every Telephone*

Your Facility Address: _(Enter Street # / Apt.#)_

(Enter City)

Nearest Main Intersection: _(Enter Street # / Apt.#)_

Your Facility Phone Number: xxx-xxx-xxxx

Contact	Phone Number
Operator	xxx-xxx-xxxx
Emergency	xxx-xxx-xxxx
Fire	xxx-xxx-xxxx
Police	xxx-xxx-xxxx
Consulting Dentist	xxx-xxx-xxxx
Poison Control	xxx-xxx-xxxx
Local Hospital Emergency Dept	xxx-xxx-xxxx
Other	xxx-xxx-xxxx
Other	xxx-xxx-xxxx

FIGURE 6–5 Emergency Contacts

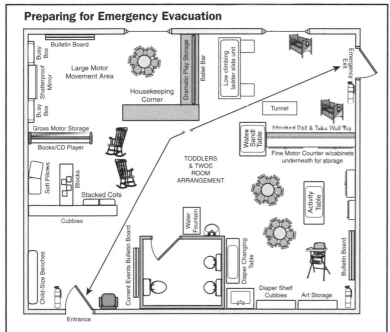

Preparing for Emergency Evacuation

Equip one or two cribs, depending on the crib size and how many children you are caring for in your group. For example, equip at least two full-size cribs with heavy caster wheels for 8–10 toddlers. Mark the beds for emergency use and place them in close proximity to the designated exit. Draw two exit routes on the emergency evacuation plan template provided. List who to call in case of fire, bomb threat, gas leak, etc. Draw on template where fire extinguisher is located. A-B-C type fire extinguishers are rated for all fires.

FIGURE 6–6 Preparing for Emergency Evacuation

Emergency Evacuation Plan

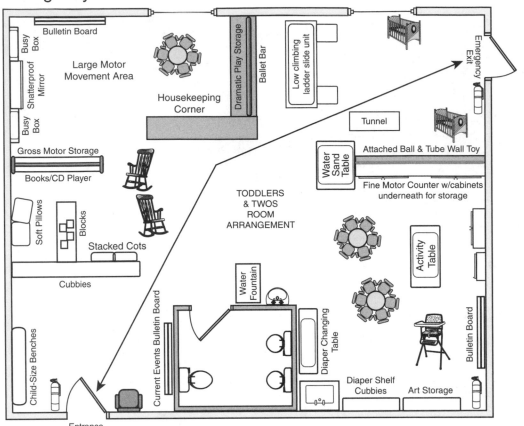

Equip one or two cribs depending on the crib size and how many children you are caring for in your group. For example, equip at least two full-size cribs with heavy caster wheels for 8–10 toddlers. Mark the beds for emergency use and place them in close proximity to the designated exit. Draw two exit routes on the emergency evacuation plan template provided. List who to call in case of fire, bomb threat, gas leak, etc. Draw on template where fire extinguisher is located. A-B-C type fire extinguishers are rated for all fires.

Center's Address: _____ *(Enter Street#/Apt.#)* _____

Nearest Main Intersection: _____ *(Enter Street#/Apt.#)* _____

Center's Phone Number: _____ xxx-xxx-xxxx _____

In Case of Fire Call: _____ xxx-xxx-xxxx _____

In Case of Bomb Threat Call: _____ xxx-xxx-xxxx _____

In Case of Gas Leak Call: _____ xxx-xxx-xxxx _____

Fire Extinguisher Expires Date: _____ *11-05-2009* _____

Emergency Bag and Blanket Are Located: _____ *in closet of main hallway* _____

Place toddlers in the emergency evacuation beds. If the door is cool, open it slowly, and make sure fire or smoke isn't blocking your escape route. If your escape is blocked, close the door and use an alternative escape route. Smoke and heat rise. Be prepared to crawl where the air is clearer and cooler near the floor. Move as far from the building as possible. In case of a real fire,

FIGURE 6–7 Emergency Evacuation Plan

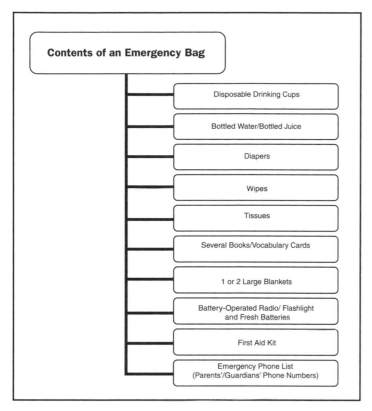

FIGURE 6-8 Emergency Bag Supplies

Hurricane Emergency Instructions

Hurricane/Tropical Storm Watch: indicates conditions are possible in the specified area within 36 hours.

Hurricane/Tropical Storm Warning: conditions are expected within 24 hours.

Send the children home.
Learn your specific evacuation route.
Secure your facility.
Close storm shutters.
Turn utilities off at main valves if instructed by authorities.
Take emergency phone numbers with you.

Your evacuation route: *turn right on West 86th Street, drive 2 blocks to*

Meridian, turn right, go 1/2 of a mile to Interstate 465 West, go for 2 miles, on 465, take the

Interstate 865 to Interstate 65 to North Carolina

FIGURE 6-9 Hurricane Emergency Instructions

Tornado Emergency Instructions

Your county or region is: _____*Marion County*_____

Tornado Watch: A tornado is possible. Remain alert for approaching storms. Tune your portable (battery-operated) radio to a local weather station.

Tornado Warning: A tornado has been sighted. Activate your emergency shelter plan immediately.

Grab your emergency bag and blanket. They are located: _____*in main hallway closet*_____

_____

Place the toddlers in the designated emergency evacuation cribs and move calmly and quickly to an interior room or hallway. Account for all children in attendance.
Your best location is: _____*Main hallway past library*_____

_____

Cover cribs with a blanket in case of flying glass or debris. Avoid windows, doors, outside walls, and corners of rooms.

FIGURE 6–10 Tornado Emergency Instructions

Earthquake Emergency Instructions

Prior to earthquakes:
- Brace high and top-heavy objects.
- Fasten cubbies, lockers, toy shelves to the wall.
- Anchor overhead lighting fixtures.
- Install flexible pipe fitting to avoid gas or water leaks.
- Know when and how to shut off electricity, gas, and water at main switches and valves.
- Locate safe spots in the room to protect yourself from dropping debris such as under a sturdy table or crib.

Your safest location is: _____*in the hallway under library tables*_____

The shutoff for gas is located: _____*in the basement next to furnace*_____

The water main is located: _____*in the kitchen next to large sink*_____

Your emergency bag is located: _____*top shelf of toy cabinet*_____

During an earthquake:

- Stay inside until shaking stops and it is safe to go outside.
- Move the toddlers to your safe location (inside a crib on an inside wall).
- Place a heavy blanket or lightweight mattress over the crib.
- If you are on the playground, move away from the building.

When the shaking stops be prepared for aftershocks. Check for injuries and administer first aid as indicated. Use flashlights if electricity is out. *Do not* light candles or matches in case of gas leakage.

FIGURE 6–11 Earthquake Emergency Instructions

Tornado/Earthquake Drill Log

Date	Time of Drill	Time Needed to Seek Cover	Comments	Full Name of Person in Charge
2/14	2:30 pm	2 minutes	Well Done!	Mrs. Ferdahard - Director

FIGURE 6–12 Tornado/Earthquake Drill Log

Building Evacuation Log

Date	Time of Drill	Evacuation Time	Comments	Full Name of Person in Charge
04-13	7:15 am	1 min 30 sec	Great Job!	Mrs. Lopez Director
05-23	12:00 pm	1 min 45 sec	Within expected time limit	Mrs. Lopez Director
06-15	2:45 pm	2 min 10 sec	Practice with New Toddler Teacher	Mrs. Lopez Director
07-30	10:45 am	1 min 50 sec	Improved time	Mrs. Lopez Director

FIGURE 6–13 Building Evacuation Log

REFERENCES

American Academy of Pediatrics, American Public Health Association, National Resource Center for Health and Safety in Child Care. *Stepping Stones to Using Caring for Our Children* (2nd ed.). (2003).

SAFE USA. Preventing childhood falls; Baby walkers. Retrieved July 14, 2002, from http://safeusa.org/falls.html

To find your specific
State's Licensing, Rules
and Regulations go to:

http://nrc.uchsc.edu

Facilitating Toddlers and Their Families

ARRIVAL: BEGINNING THE DAY

Everyone appreciates a warm welcome upon arrival. Make an effort to greet your children and their families as they arrive. At this age, many toddlers experience separation anxiety and stranger anxiety. During this phase it is sometimes difficult for toddlers to allow their parents or guardians to leave without tears. Every parent and child have their own style for sharing a good-bye. Some parents will appreciate if you take their children so they can leave. Others will spend time with their children hanging up their belongings, settling them at the breakfast table, or selecting a toy they will enjoy. It is important to determine with parents how you can best assist with the morning arrival and a smooth separation.

Collecting pertinent information during morning arrival allows the teachers to provide appropriate care for each toddler. An example of a Beginning Our Day sheet can be found in Figure 7–1. Make a copy of the Beginning Our Day template in the Forms and Templates appendix to gather pertinent information from the parents about the toddlers' most recent activity such as the time they awoke, when they ate their last meal or snack, when they received their last diaper change, and any other information that could assist with specific care that day. Morning arrivals are a very busy time. Place the Beginning Our Day sheet on a clipboard near the Daily Medication Sheet (Figure 5–1) in an area easily accessible to the parent for convenient recording.

DAILY TODDLER SCHEDULE OUTLINE

Examples of two different Daily Toddler Schedule Outlines are provided in Chapter 3, "Establishing an Excellent Path for Communication." One example provides a schedule that allows for one nap, and the other allows for two naps. Typically one-year-olds start out with a morning and afternoon nap and gradually adopt a one-nap schedule in the latter half of their second year. As you will note in this example, the daily schedule outline only *briefly* lists the day's planned activities with the corresponding times noted, but does not offer any specific details. This schedule is primarily used for a quick overview and reference for the toddlers' planned day. You will also be asked to complete a *detailed* daily schedule.

Typically the Daily Toddler Schedule Outline is updated at least every season, especially in climates where the balance of indoor and outdoor activities changes seasonally due to rough weather. The Forms and Templates Appendix includes a template for creating your own Daily Toddler Schedule Outline. Fill in the blanks to reflect the typical schedule you have developed for the toddlers you care for. Maintain this schedule so it always provides a substitute or assistant teacher with a current version of the toddlers' planned day.

Beginning Our Day   Date: _July 8_
Welcome

Child's Name	Time Awoke	Last Meal/Snack	Last Diaper Change or Toilet Break	Comments, if any
Erica (Enter Last Name)	5:30 am	Breakfast	5:45 am	Dr. appt. will pick up at 2
Lisa (Enter Last Name)	6:00 am	Juice	6:15 am	
Ethan (Enter Last Name)	7:00 am	Graham crackers	7:15 am	
Harriet (Enter Last Name)	7:15 am		7:40 am	Meeting downtown Ms. Smith 848-5267
Carter (Enter Last Name)	6 ish	Bottle	6:15 am	Up early – probably tired
Jack (Enter Last Name)	8:30 am		8:45 am	
Paul (Enter Last Name)	6:50 am	Muffin	7:15 am	May want more breakfast
Charmaine (Enter Last Name)	7:45 am	Juice	8:00 am	Teething/bottom red
Tosha (Enter Last Name)	5:45 am	Breakfast	6:00 am	Grandpa Brown will pick up today
Annette (Enter Last Name)	7:30 am	Dinner	7:45 am	Hungry

FIGURE 7–1 Beginning Our Day Log

TODDLER CLASSROOM SCHEDULE DETAILS

Two different examples of Daily Toddler Schedule Details are provided in Chapter 3, "Establishing an Excellent Path for Communication." One example provides a schedule that allows for one nap, and the other allows for two naps. Detailed descriptions of the daily activities are outlined here, as well as specific information such as "Jack and Lisa eat breakfast every day" or "Max has a milk allergy." Describe the children's whole day. The information provided *in detail* will ensure that, in your absence, the toddlers will experience the familiar routines you have established and will certainly provide the substitute teacher with the confidence needed to fulfill his or her tasks.

A Daily Toddler Schedule Details template for your use can be found in the Forms and Templates Appendix. Make a duplicate and fill in the blanks to accurately reflect the detailed schedule you have planned for your group of toddlers.

LESSON PLANS

Once the Daily Toddler Schedule Details are completed, the weekly lesson plan is the next endeavor. An example of Toddler Weekly Lesson Plans is provided in Figure 7–2. Lesson plans are your blueprint for each day. Lesson planning is a crucial element for providing a

Stage of Play Development: Egocentric/Parallel

Toddler Weekly Lesson Plans

Week of: Jan 3-9 **Group Name:** Blueberries **Theme:** Winter **Lead Caregiver:** Ms. Karen

Activities	Sun	Mon	Tues	Wed	Thurs	Fri	Sat
Concept		Signs of Winter	Plants & Animals	What We Wear	Winter Activities	Winter Magic	
Sharing Time		Talk about signs of winter	This is how the wind blows	My coat, my hat, my mittens	Sledding, igloos, snowballs	I am hot / I am cold	
Language Skills							
KIDEX: The Music of Sound Activities		19-21 I-G Puppet talks about winter	16-18 I-C Noisemaker rhythms	19-21 I-D Sing "Did You Ever See a Snowman"	22-24 I-M Musical instruments	13-14 I-A Winter picture words	
Songs/Finger plays		"I'm a Little Ice Cube"	Pictures of animals that hibernate	"3 Little Kittens Lost Their Mittens"	"Frosty the Snowman"	"Are You Sleeping, Little Bear?" (song)	
Reading/Stories (Flannel Board/Vocabulary/Puppets)		Dear Rebecca, Winter's Here	A Hat for Minerva	Br-r-r-r	Katy and the Big Snow	Prize in the Snow	
Fine Motor Manipulation		Snap & button	Brush & comb our hair	Dump & load the "snow" blocks	Practice zipping	Stacking rings	
Cognitive/Sensory/Pre-Math/Science		Line up our boots or shoes	The plants, trees, and animals are asleep	Match the mittens	Different colored hats	Float ice cubes in water table	
KIDEX: Life is Interesting & My World Activities		13-15 3-L Weather outside	13-15 3-J Hang bird feeder & watch	19-21 4-A Gelatin blocks	16-18 4-A Fragrant snow balls cotton	22-24 2-L Winter puzzles	
Arts Exploration/Crafts		Paint with sponges	Make peanut butter bird feeder	Color with white crayon on dark paper	Finger paint with pudding	Black constr. paper / white chalk	
Gross Motor							
KIDEX: My Body Is Wonderful Activities		13-15 2-A Walk on snow (cushions)	19-21 2-I Riding toys (sleigh ride)	19-21 2-F Catch the snowflakes (bubbles)	16-18 2-H March to winter music	16-18 2-H Sleigh ride in a box (scooting)	
Indoor/Outdoor Activities		Toss snowballs in big basket (rolled socks)	Throw snowballs (ping pong ball)	Scarf dance	Roll the big snowball (ball)	Make pretend snow angels & ice skate	

Daily Play Centers

- Housekeeping/Dramatic Play/Toys Center
- Fine Motor/Art/Eating/Water Table
- Active Play/Music Movement/Toys
- Library/Music/Quiet Play/Block Center/Computer

Self Help Skills/Social Skills

13–24 Months — Integrate and encourage the development of skills during this 12-month span

- Put on and remove shoes & socks with help
- Wash & dry hands
- Feed self/rudimentary use of fork & spoon
- Potty training practice (18 months & older only)
- Help with cleanup
- Practice yes & no
- Practice please & thank you
- Body/self-awareness
- Safety awareness
- Follow basic instructions

FIGURE 7–2 Toddler Weekly Lesson Plans

rich environment and a satisfying experience for the toddlers you care for. A Toddler Weekly Lesson Plans template has been provided in the Forms and Templates appendix. Use this template to create lesson plans for the toddler group. Many books are available to assist with lesson plan ideas. Check the resource guide for a list.

Keep a copy of your current lesson plan handy in the KIDEX Class Book for you and all staff members who care for the children to refer to. Toddlers aren't yet able to discuss their day with their parents, so post the lesson plan on the Current Events Bulletin Board or somewhere equally visible to the parents.

TODDLER DAILY OBSERVATION SHEET

In Chapter 3, "Establishing an Excellent Path for Communication," a completed example of the Toddler Daily Observation Sheet is provided. You will find a blank template of the Toddler Daily Observation Sheet in the Forms and Templates Appendix. Keep a written daily record for each toddler. Accurate recording in a timely manner gives the family a clear understanding of their child's day. Adopting a routine for recording ensures all important aspects are covered. Provide the parents with a copy of this record so they too will have a record of their child's napping patterns, toileting patterns or diaper changes, eating patterns, and overall mood and activity level for the day.

Consider using two-part forms for the Toddler Daily Observation Sheet. Provide the parents/guardians with one at departure. File the second copy for at least a couple of months, or longer if your state requires it. It is very helpful to have written observation documents to review if a conference is warranted. Occasionally parents/guardians express concerns: for example, a toddler's appetite may seem to fluctuate and the family might want to know how much the child is eating at the center. These documents arm you with the information needed to answer a family's concerns and reach an agreeable outcome. The director is encouraged to review all records at least monthly to look for consistent recording practices or spot areas in which intervention or education is warranted. Before you leave for lunch or at the end of your shift, check the charts for accuracy. Remember: after your shift ends, your written observations provide pertinent information for parents' questions regarding their child's care. An accurate record is essential to facilitate open communication!

LANGUAGE BUILDING, READING, AND SINGING

Children learn language by listening to the sounds other people make. They need to hear talking and the use of descriptive language around them. Use a variety of means to expose toddlers to language. Short stories are found in books such as *5-Minute Fairy Tales* (1999), written by Publications International. Picture books and vocabulary cards with pictures can be found in most education and toy stores such as United Art and Education, 800-322-3247 or http://www.UnitedNow.com. Young children particularly enjoy flannel board stories. The stories are complemented with flannel pieces that bring the story alive and allow the toddlers to participate easily. You can also cut pictures from magazines and place them in a Plexiglas display board, found in school supply catalogs, that attaches to the wall. Change the picture selections on a regular basis. Hang pictures or vocabulary cards by the diaper changing station.

Make a habit of describing your actions to the toddlers as well as the emotions and feelings they exhibit. For instance, a toddler might cry because he or she is frustrated that a puzzle piece won't fit. Respond with, "Yes, it is frustrating when things don't fit. Try this hole." Toddlers understand spoken words far sooner than they master the ability to speak themselves. It can be a source of great frustration to lack the skills needed to communicate an immediate need or desire. It is helpful at times to ask children to "show me" if they are trying to communicate a yearning without success.

Reading to children for as little as 15–20 minutes per day from an early age contributes to positive brain development. Simple books with pictures and photos allow children to read stories to themselves. Provide them with sturdy books made of heavy cardboard (board books). Stories with rhyming words and repetitive phrases appeal to young children. There is a vast selection of books available. Many centers have access to public libraries and "Bookmobile programs" that come to the child care site.

Singing and playing songs on a regular basis is yet another excellent opportunity for practicing language skills. Nursery rhymes are also enjoyable. Many nursery rhymes are very old, dating as far back as the fourteenth century. There are a multitude of nursery rhyme books to be found in libraries and bookstores. An extensive list of the most popular nursery rhymes appears on "Lost Lyrics of Old Nursery Rhymes: 112 Additional Online Nursery Rhymes, History and their Origins!" (http://www.rhymes.org.uk).

TRACKING DEVELOPMENTAL MILESTONES

Figures 7–3, 7–4, 7–5, and 7–6 provide a guide for observing and recording developmental milestones for each toddler. Observe the toddler's behaviors at each of the age ranges.

1. Check the behaviors with a Y for yes if the child demonstrates this action regularly.

2. Mark S for sometimes if the toddler is just beginning to demonstrate the behavior or only does it sometimes.

3. Mark N for not yet if the toddler doesn't demonstrate this action yet. Use the listed developments as a guide for observing.

4. Place the current age range on an individual clipboard for each child with the Activities and Play Opportunities, Toddler's Individual Monthly Profile, and Toddler Daily Observation Checklist for handy reference when time permits. (See Chapter 3, Figure 3–16)

It is very important to understand from the beginning that children will develop at similar rates but each in a unique pattern. Blank Developmental Milestones pages can be found in the Forms and Templates appendix.

All children are individuals. They each have their own unique personalities so consequently they will each develop at a slightly different pace. The checklist provided is a broad list suggesting approximate developmental milestones that can be expected as outlined for each few months. If you find a toddler is not exhibiting the majority of characteristics listed, there could be many reasons. For instance, if the child was born prematurely then he or she would not be expected to follow the average suggested milestones and might lag a few weeks behind. A child who is reserved might avoid certain activities but not necessarily to his or her detriment. If you have a child who consistently does not exhibit signs of achieving the majority of the outlined milestones, with a lag of five to seven weeks, then perhaps more exploration is in order; share your concerns with the director or program supervisor for consideration.

Review the developmental milestones when a child reaches the beginning of the age range. Complete the checklist at the end of the age range. Completing it at the end of the age range provides the toddler time to achieve mastery of each skill outlined.

13–15 Months
DEVELOPMENTAL MILESTONES

TODDLERS CAN:

___Y___ PULL UP TO A STANDING POSITION

___Y___ MOVE FROM PLACE TO PLACE, HOLDING ON FOR BALANCE

___Y___ EXPLORE, VERY CURIOUS

___Y___ PUT OBJECTS INTO A CONTAINER

___Y___ IMITATE ACTIVITIES DEMONSTRATED

___Y___ USE 1 or 2 RECOGNIZABLE WORDS

___Y___ BEGIN TO DRINK FROM A CUP

___S___ BEGIN TO RECOGNIZE AND IDENTIFY OWN BODY PARTS

___Y___ USE SOME GESTURES SUCH AS WAVING

___Y___ USE WORDS LIKE *MA-MA* OR *DA-DA* INTENTIONALLY

___Y___ BEND OVER AND PICK UP AN OBJECT

___Y___ BEGIN TO ATTEMPT WALKING

___Y___ WALK UP STEPS WITH HELP

___S___ USES 3 to 6 WORDS

___Y___ BUILD A TOWER OF 2 CUBES

___Y___ IMITATE DUMPING OBJECTS

___Y___ UNDERSTAND A FEW WORDS

___N___ WALK UNAIDED

___S___ FIT ROUND BLOCK IN A ROUND HOLE

___S___ DRINK FROM A CUP UNASSISTED

___Y___ POINT TO A DESIRED OBJECT

___S___ PUSH, PULL, OR CARRY TOYS WHILE WALKING

___Y___ ENJOY LOOKING AT BOOKS

___Y___ SCRIBBLE WITH CRAYON

___Y___ USE A SPOON INTERMITTENTLY

> *Important Note: children will develop at similar rates but each in a unique pattern. If you find a child is not exhibiting the majority of characteristics listed, there could be many plausible reasons ranging from premature birth to a more reserved and cautious personality. This list is a broad overview and not inclusive of all developmental milestones toddlers will experience.*

TODDLER _Janelle (Enter Last Name)_ CAREGIVER ___Ms. Laurence___ DATE ___7/12___

Y = YES	S = SOMETIMES	N = NOT YET

FIGURE 7–3 13–15 Months Developmental Milestones

16-18 Months

DEVELOPMENTAL MILESTONES

TODDLERS CAN:

___Y___ IMITATE ACTIVITIES AND BEHAVIORS

___Y___ ROLL A BALL

___Y___ IMITATE FEEDING A DOLL OR SOFT TOY

___Y___ TURNS 2 or 3 PAGES AT A TIME

___Y___ HAND A TOY TO SOMEONE

___Y___ FIND A BALL THAT ROLLS OUT OF SIGHT

___Y___ PLAY A SIMPLE MUSICAL INSTRUMENT (SPOON & PAN)

___Y___ USE SOME WORDS CORRECTLY, SUCH AS *MA-MA, OH-OH, BYE-BYE*

___Y___ LATCH ONTO AT LEAST ONE COMFORT HABIT OR OBJECT

___Y___ BUILDS 2–4 CUBE TOWER

___Y___ ATTEMPT TO KICK A BALL

___Y___ BEGIN TO COMBINE WORDS

___S___ REMOVE AN ARTICLE OF CLOTHING

___S___ UNDERSTAND MANY WORDS AND SIMPLE DIRECTIONS

___Y___ BEGIN TO THROW A BALL OVERHEAD

___Y___ TRY TO SING SONGS

___S___ POINT AT AND NAME FAMILIAR THINGS

___Y___ MATCH SAME TOYS

___Y___ USE SPOON AND FORK BUT NOT EXCLUSIVELY

___S___ BEGIN TO ASSIST WITH TOY CLEANUP

___Y___ PUT UP TO SIX LARGE PEGS INTO A PEGBOARD

___N___ ATTEMPT TO JUMP WITH BOTH FEET

___Y___ FEEL FRUSTRATED EASILY WHEN OVERWHELMED

> *Important Note: children will develop at similar rates but each in a unique pattern. If you find a child is not exhibiting the majority of characteristics listed, there could be many plausible reasons ranging from premature birth to a more reserved and cautious personality. This list is a broad overview and not inclusive of all developmental milestones toddlers will experience.*

TODDLER *Maria (Enter Last Name)* CAREGIVER *Ms. Franklin*		DATE *4/5*
Y = YES	S = SOMETIMES	N = NOT YET

FIGURE 7–4 16–18 Months Developmental Milestones

19-21 Months

DEVELOPMENTAL MILESTONES

TODDLERS CAN:

__Y__ ZIP AND UNZIP EASY ZIPPERS WITH ASSISTANCE

__Y__ SHOW MANY EMOTIONS

__S__ EXPERIENCE STRANGER ANXIETY OR SHY BEHAVIOR IN NEW CIRCUMSTANCES

__Y__ ATTEMPT TO CLAP HANDS TO RHYTHMS

__Y__ CHATTER MANY WORDS OFTEN MISPRONOUNCED

__Y__ USE A COUPLE DOZEN WORDS REGULARLY

__Y__ OFTEN USE NONVERBAL LANGUAGE TO COMMUNICATE

__Y__ UNDERSTAND SIMPLE INSTRUCTIONS

__S__ COPY HOUSEWORK

__Y__ WASH AND DRY HANDS WITH HELP

__Y__ USE 50-PLUS SINGLE WORDS

__Y__ BUILD A TOWER OF 4–6 CUBES

__Y__ ENJOY SONGS, NURSERY RHYMES, & FINGER PLAYS

__Y__ BEGIN TO COMBINE WORDS

__S__ SPILL DRINK FREQUENTLY

__Y__ ENJOY PLAY DOUGH, PAINT, PAPER, AND CRAYONS

__Y__ RIDE SMALL RIDING TOYS WITHOUT PEDALS

__Y__ TURN FAMILIAR PICTURES RIGHT SIDE UP

__Y__ USE HER OR HIS OWN NAME

__S__ BEGIN TO PUT ON ONE ARTICLE OF CLOTHING

__Y__ KICK A BALL FORWARD

__Y__ COMBINE WORDS

> *Important Note: children will develop at similar rates but each in a unique pattern. If you find a child is not exhibiting the majority of characteristics listed, there could be many plausible reasons ranging from premature birth to a more reserved and cautious personality. This list is a broad overview and not inclusive of all developmental milestones toddlers will experience.*

TODDLER _Jacob (Enter Last Name)_ CAREGIVER _Ms. Everette_ DATE _10/15_

| Y = YES | S = SOMETIMES | N = NOT YET |

FIGURE 7–5 19–21 Months Developmental Milestones

22-24 Months

DEVELOPMENTAL MILESTONES

TODDLERS CAN:

_S_ STRING LARGE BEADS

_Y_ UNWRAP PACKAGES, ONCE STARTED

_Y_ JUMP UP

_Y_ WALK UP STEPS

_S_ BEGIN LEARNING GENTLE TOUCHING OF FRAGILE OBJECTS

_Y_ MATCH SOUNDS TO ANIMALS

_Y_ LISTEN TO SHORT STORIES

_S_ RUN FAST

_Y_ BEGIN TO COMFORT OTHERS

_Y_ RECOGNIZE SELF IN A PHOTOGRAPH

_Y_ USE SHORT SENTENCES

_S_ BEGIN USING PREPOSITIONS SUCH AS: _BY, IN, TO, OF_

_Y_ TURN ONE PAGE AT A TIME (REFINED PINCER GRASP)

_Y_ LOVE SOUND OF VOICE, ENJOY NOISY OUTBURSTS

_Y_ ENJOY WATER AND SAND PLAY

_Y_ SING SOME WORDS TO SOME SONGS

_N_ BEGIN USING PRONOUNS SUCH AS _I_ AND _ME_

_Y_ BUILD A TOWER OF 6–8 CUBES

_Y_ CARRY ON A CONVERSATION WITH 2 or 3 SENTENCES

_Y_ COPY FOUR WORDS YOU SAY

_Y_ SPEAK AND BE UNDERSTOOD HALF THE TIME

_Y_ ASSEMBLE A 1–3 PIECE PUZZLE

_Y_ DISTINGUISH BETWEEN "YOURS" AND "MINE"

> _Important Note: children will develop at similar rates but each in a unique pattern. If you find a child is not exhibiting the majority of characteristics listed, there could be many plausible reasons ranging from premature birth to a more reserved and cautious personality. This list is a broad overview and not inclusive of all developmental milestones toddlers will experience._

TODDLER _Elizabeth (Enter Last Name)_ CAREGIVER _Ms. Luck_ DATE _9/16_

Y = YES	S = SOMETIMES	N = NOT YET

FIGURE 7–6 22–24 Months Developmental Milestones

PLANNING ACTIVITIES AND PLAY OPPORTUNITIES

Toddlers are hard workers. They learn many new skills each month. In order to achieve mastery of each skill, they must be provided with various play opportunities for practice. Since each child develops at his or her own pace, familiarize yourself with activities that are appropriate for each month of development (see Figures 7–7, 7–8, 7–9, and 7–10). Providing a variety of activities will assist a child to build large and small muscle control, language skills, sensory responses, mental cognition, and social growth. The activities and play opportunities listed provide a variety of experiences in four areas. Choose activities from all four categories. *The Music of Sound* offers opportunities to explore sound, music, reading, pictures, and singing to assist with building and mastering language skills. *My Body is Wonderful* encourages the toddlers' budding fine motor and gross physical skills. The activities provide practice in refining their rapidly developing mobility. Activities listed in *My World* and *Life Is Interesting* provide for sensory and creative play that will entice toddlers to experience and explore the world they live in.

Figure 7–11 provides recipes to make flavored play dough, gelatin blocks, and large ice cubes.

PERSONAL SUPPLY INVENTORY CHECKLIST

Toddlers require plenty of supplies! If your center depends on the children's families to provide supplies, use the Personal Supply Inventory Checklist to communicate when supplies need replenishing (see Figure 7–12). Form a habit of reporting the individual inventory once a week. Notify your clients when a child's supplies are low. Planning ahead will decrease the inconvenience caused by completely depleting needed supplies. Routinely inventory supplies on Thursday or Friday; this allows busy families to shop over the weekend.

DEPARTURE: ENDING THE DAY WITH EACH TODDLER

Upon departure there are many details to attend to. Assist the parents or guardians in gathering each child's personal belongings, such as soiled clothing, medications, ointments, and blankets, thus promoting a pleasant transition. If time permits, briefly review the Toddler Daily Observation Sheet with them and add any special observations you might have noted that day. Provide the parents with a copy of this record so they too will have a record of their child's napping patterns, toileting patterns or diaper changes, eating patterns, and overall mood and activity level. As you are well aware, toddlers require a great deal of time and energy. The parents have often spent a long day fulfilling career obligations. Although they are very pleased to see their child, they often have an accumulation of stress from their day. Your pleasant attitude and helpful manner assisting them to leave the center smoothly will be greatly appreciated. As you bring your day to a close, take a few moments to appreciate yourself for all of the significant efforts and lasting contributions you have made in these children's lives.

13-15 Months

ALL ACTIVITIES 2–10 MINUTES

Category 1	**THE MUSIC OF SOUND** **(Sound/Language/Verbal Practice)** • Name things in picture books • Point to and name body parts • Sing "This is the way we wash our face... Comb our hair... Brush our teeth..." • Sing and play "Pat-a-Cake" • Play with a musical jack in the box • Sing "Itsy Bitsy Spider" • Have toddler point to the pictures of animals that you name • Sing Jack and Jill • Use contact paper-covered photos to talk about things a toddler sees every day • Play with xylophone • Use picture books at storytime • Play with spoons and metal pans to build rhythm & sound skills • Look at & discuss old magazines or toy catalogues (replace torn ones to avoid choking from ripped paper) • Tape contact paper-covered pictures up for toddler to look at • Listen to lullaby music during quiet time
Category 2	**MY BODY IS WONDERFUL** **(Large/Fine Motor/Self-Exploration Practice)** • Practice walking—hold child's hand, try different surfaces • Provide push toys such as a toy grocery cart and a baby buggy • Drop wooden clothes pins into a container • Practice stacking with stacking rings • Roll child a ball and encourage child to pick it up and return it to you • Provide child with a bucket filled with plastic blocks for dumping & filling • Mount busy box to wall for busy box play time • At snack time, put oyster crackers in a paper cup to practice picking up small objects • Ask where your nose, eyes, ears, etc. are • Practice hugging and say "Oh, what a nice hug!" • Provide pull toys to pull around the room • Play with a big beach ball

Toddler's Name: _Makalani (Enter Last Name)_ Caregiver: _Ms. Rogers_

Date Initiated: _2/11_ Date Completed: _3/15_

FIGURE 7–7 13–15 Months Activities

Continued 13–15 Months Activities

Category **3**	**MY WORLD** **(Exploring/Emotions/Science/Pre-math Practice)** • Provide a noisemaker for shaking • Blow bubbles and have toddler pop them • Go for a walk and point out different sounds, or use the "see & say" method • Tape contact paper to the wall sticky side out & give toddlers object to stick to it • Practice hanging objects up on hooks attached to a hook board • Paste different leaves on paper and cover with contact paper to talk about • Take special walks as each season changes and talk about each new season • Put ice cubes made from a large container in a water table • Bring out a different animal each week to practice its name • Set up bird feeder outside and watch it through the window • Match pictures in plastic containers with real objects such as keys, a spoon, a ball, a fish, etc. • Look out the window and talk about the weather outside • Fill a plastic can with plastic rings to sort & dump • Take a walk and feel the bark on the trees • Listen to a tape of different weather sounds
Category **4**	**LIFE IS INTERESTING** **(Tactile/Cognitive/Touching Practice)** • Use one fat crayon to scribble on a big sheet of paper • Color on dark construction paper with nontoxic colored chalk • Introduce nontoxic finger painting with one color • Give 6" piece masking tape–show places to stick • Fill a pan with a small amount of water and provide a sponge to dip & explore • Provide several sets of nesting blocks to practice stacking • Fill a plastic pop bottle with water, oil, & food coloring, glue cap on securely, and explore • Provide colorful fabric swatches to place on contact paper • Use a colored scarf to hide behind and play peekaboo • Fill a container with cold spaghetti and explore • Make a large scribble book • Call mommy, daddy, or grandparents at work on play telephone • Put out hats to try on and look at in the mirror • Match tools to their silhouettes • Cover a table with taped down paper and finger paint with pudding

Toddler's Name: _Makalani (Enter Last Name)_ Caregiver: _Ms. Rogers_

Date Initiated: _2/11_ Date Completed: _3/15_

FIGURE 7–7 13–15 Months Activities *(Continued)*

16-18 Months

ALL ACTIVITIES 2-15 MINUTES

Category 1	**THE MUSIC OF SOUND** **(Sound/Language/Verbal Practice)** • Look at animal pictures, make appropriate sounds & encourage imitation • Play music with baby rattles while marching to the sound • Fill a 1/2 gallon jug with 3/4 cup dry beans, glue lid on, and shake to make a great noise maker • Practice "what is this?" by pointing & asking • Play nursery song music • Pull toys out of a box and ask toddler what they are • Use felt pieces for story time–have toddler put the pieces on the board • Help toddlers understand their emotions by describing their feelings • Sing "Where Is Thumpkin?" • Practice language at the table by asking, "Where is your bib?", "cup?", "plate?" etc. • Sing nursery songs & keep rhythm with musical sticks • Look at & talk about book of colors • Play with different size bells & chimes • Ask toddler to bring to you items in the room that you request • Play lively music and dance to it
Category 2	**MY BODY IS WONDERFUL** **(Large/Fine Motor/Self-Exploration Practice)** • March to band music • Act out "Pop goes the weasel" • Hang a beach ball from the ceiling in a cloth bag to use for punching • Provide several large boxes for toddler to play in • Throw wads of paper into a wide basket • Show how to kick with a large, soft ball • Put tennis balls in a hat, put the hat on, and have fun chasing the balls that fall out • Provide boxes to push around the room • Place a 7"-12" wide flat board on the ground to walk on • Practice jumping off of carpet squares • Push plastic curlers through matching egg carton holes • Put out large pegs and pegboards for matching practice • Play with large stacking blocks

Toddler's Name: _Cecilia (Enter Last Name)_   Caregiver: _Ms. Krueger_

Date Initiated: _5/7_   Date Completed: _6/2_

FIGURE 7-8 16-18 Months Activities

Continued 16–18 Months Activities

Category **3**	**MY WORLD** **(Exploring/Emotions/Science/Pre-math Practice)** • Blow air through a straw so toddler can feel the "wind" • Make a "noisy" book out of wax paper—glue pictures of various animals • Bring flowers to touch & smell under supervision • Hang up pictures of dogs & cats to look at • Sit on a blanket inside or outside for story time • Look in a mirror and make faces—encourage toddler to copy you • Sit on big blanket outside while eating snack • Put pictures of tropical fish in a magnetic photo book to look at • Play scoop & pour with oatmeal or sand outdoors • Bring in toddler-friendly animals for a short visit • Provide wet sponges to wash toys • Put a blanket & toys in the shade, in the sun, and indoors on rainy days, and talk about each environment • Collect a bug in a plastic jar for toddler to watch • Provide a goldfish to watch • Talk about happy, sad, angry, and frightened • Put chairs in a single file, sit toddler on each chair & take an imaginary bus ride
Category **4**	**LIFE IS INTERESTING** **(Tactile/Cognitive/Touching Practice)** • Smell 3 or 4 different fragrances found on cotton balls, inside of plastic salt & pepper shakers • Make milk shakes together for an afternoon snack • Tape drawing paper over sandpaper for textured scribble • Give each toddler a pan full of 2" blocks to dump & fill • Give each toddler a purse: demo how to fill, dump, and carry their treasures • Tape paper over netting material for textured scribble • Wash dishes with soapy water in a water table • Explore sandpaper, velvet, and satin for rough, soft, and smooth textures • Make a ramp from 3"–4" wide board to run cars down • Set out dolls in dishpans with blankets for each toddler • Set table with dishes & pretend kitchen items • Wash baby dolls with several dishpans of water (1" deep water only) • Use glue & glitter to decorate pictures (e.g., snowflakes, leaves, fish, flowers) • Play with sorting cubes • Bring in fist-size rocks, smooth & rough, and explore

Toddler's Name: ___Cecilia (Enter Last Name)___ Caregiver: ___Ms. Krueger___

Date Initiated: ___5/7___ Date Completed: ___6/2___

FIGURE 7–8 16–18 Months Activities *(Continued)*

19–21 Months

ALL ACTIVITIES 5–20 MINUTES

Category 1	**THE MUSIC OF SOUND** **(Sound/Language/Verbal Practice)** • Play with a variety of musical instruments • Use puppets to practice children's names • Help describe words to toddler that express happy feelings • Sing "Did You Ever See a Lassie" • Darken the room & describe things you see with a flashlight • Help toddler describe frustrating feelings using words • Use puppets to practice different vocabulary words • Copy sounds you hear such as cars and planes and encourage toddler to repeat • Read books about people who work such as doctors, firefighters, police officers, etc. • Hold baby dolls and/or stuffed animals while singing "Rock-a-Bye Baby" • Explore loud & soft sounds with musical instruments • "Open, shut them," finger play • Sing nursery rhymes • Tape-record toddlers' voices and play back • Play a tape with different kinds of transportation sounds
Category 2	**MY BODY IS WONDERFUL** **(Large/Fine Motor/Self-Exploration Practice)** • Give toddler a soft animal or doll to carry on your walk • Play with zippers • Play with pop beads • Play with large blocks for stacking • Crawl around and pretend to be different animals • Fill a paper cup with shaving cream & have toddler spread it on a tray • Build with large bristle blocks or duplo blocks • Brush or comb a doll's or stuffed animal's hair with a comb or brush • Provide riding toys without pedals • Practice rolling different size balls to toddler • Put a small toy in a large, empty matchbox and show how to open it • Stick a piece of masking tape on toddler's clothing and practice peeling it off

Toddler's Name: _Chris (Enter Last Name)_   Caregiver: _Ms. Donahue_

Date Initiated: _11/6_   Date Completed: _12/22_

FIGURE 7–9 19–21 Months Activities

Continued 19–21 Months Activities

Category 3	**MY WORLD** **(Exploring/Emotions/Science/Pre-Math Practice)** • Blow bubbles in pan of water with straws—put a hole in the straw to avoid sucking • Take a walk & say words for as many things that you see as you can • Hang "wind sock" outside of window & talk about the wind • Hang up pictures of different kinds of transportation • Lie on the floor and make pretend snow angels • Lie on your back and look at the clouds or pictures on the ceiling • Provide a small amount of water & sponges to wash furniture • Take a walk inside and outside to feel the different textures • Look at pictures of different kinds of horses • Play with 2-piece puzzles of animals made from cutting pictures in two • Bring different size feathers to the room to explore • Play with bubble blowing outside • Bring to a petting zoo or explore zoo animals with a book • Read stories about the seasons • Practice laughing—explore pictures of toddlers having fun
Category 4	**LIFE IS INTERESTING** **(Tactile/Cognitive/Touching Practice)** • Make flavored play dough—use while warm! • Put string (no longer than 12" long) around stuffed animals and use to pull animals around and to pretend walking a pet • Paint with sand & paint on construction paper • Spread peanut butter on crackers for snacks • Glue packing peanuts to a picture and paint to make packing peanut picture • Provide dress-up clothes for pretend dress-up • Put out a pile of large socks and practice putting them on • Finger paint on paper plates • Match colors with mittens, socks, or flowers) • Play store with used food boxes • Use different colored water markers to draw with; finger paint a picture of a pig with mud • Play with gelatin blocks • Color a flower and glue a perfumed cotton ball in the middle of it • Taste different flavors: pickles, lemon, ice cream • Sprinkle sand on pictures prepped with glue

Toddler's Name: _____*Chris (Enter Last Name)*_____ Caregiver: _____*Ms. Donahue*_____

Date Initiated: _____*11/6*_____ Date Completed: _____*12/22*___

Figure 7–9 19–21 Months Activities *(Continued)*

22-24 Months

ALL ACTIVITIES 5–20 MINUTES

Category 1	**THE MUSIC OF SOUND** **(Sound/Language/Verbal Practice)** • Sing "Rain Rain Go Away"—use gestures • Practice everyone's name—have each toddler say his or her name • Sing "Old McDonald" and point out animals in a picture book • Read nursery rhymes at story time • Explore object flash cards • Play teddy bear, teddy bear • Practice saying 3 or 4 words at a time and then have toddler repeat • Tape family members on each finger and sing "Where is...?" • Sing "This Is the Way We Wash Our Clothes" • Look at and discuss a Richard Scarry book like *Things That Go* • Sing "The Wheels On the Bus" • Have a puppet point out objects for toddler to name • Play musical instruments • Talk about family members • Roll ball to toddler and say child's full name
Category 2	**MY BODY IS WONDERFUL** **(Large/Fine Motor/Self-Exploration Practice)** • Practice understanding gentle touching of friends & fragile things • Use small, low slide—assist with sliding • Use a sponge to squeeze water out into a bowl & then pick the water back up with a sponge • Cut large straws in thirds—lace with shoe lace • Practice screwing lids on plastic jars • Play follow the leader with cheerful music playing • Take shoes off, sit, and practice touching your toes • Roll small cars through a paper towel tube • Put long pieces of masking tape on the floor and practice stepping over the tape • Practice standing on one foot at a time • String large beads w/ a shoelace (wrap ends with masking tape) • Play with 2–4 piece puzzles

Toddler's Name: _____Ben (Enter Last Name)_____ Caregiver: _____Ms. Hill_____

Date Initiated: _____6/23_____ Date Completed: _____7/16_____

FIGURE 7–10 22–24 Months Activities

Continued 22–24 Months Activities

Category **3**	**MY WORLD** **(Exploring/Emotions/Science/Pre-math Practice)** • Explore different size/shape shells (use a safe size) • Make a large ice cube in a milk carton to explore during water table time • Bring different types of tree leaves in to feel • Play a tape that explores different water sounds • Hang up pictures of different farm animals • Use big tweezers to transfer small objects into different containers • Explore the feel & shape of pine cones • Play a tape that explores different insects like crickets • Dance outdoors or indoors with scarves & animals • Hang up pictures of the sun & the moon • Put oatmeal or cornmeal in the water table to play with • Take walking excursion and provide a pretend camera to photograph with • Use imitation play—toddler start as seed, then the teacher waters the seed, the seed grows into a plant and moves with the wind • Dance outdoors or indoors with scarves & stuffed animals • Explore things that open & shut • Practice "helping" a sad stuffed animal friend
Category **4**	**LIFE IS INTERESTING** **(Tactile/Cognitive/Touching Practice)** • Paint with water pictures or use a brush & water on a side wall • Dress stuffed animals with large t-shirts & hats • Make binoculars from toilet paper rolls & decorate • Explore hot & cold—what different textures do we feel? Soft, hard, etc. • Go to a restaurant, take pretend orders and eat pretend food • Make masks out of paper plates, cut holes for eyes, and look in the mirror • Practice dressing dolls • Fingerpaint with different colors on an individual square, then make a class quilt • Decorate sugar cookies to eat for snack • Play follow the leader • Set up play areas and when interested toddlers join in, move on to set up new areas • Practice ripping up old magazines • Use pieces of fruit like a ½ orange or a cucumber to put in paint and stamp onto paper • Trace each hand, color, and add names to each finger to build a name tree • Paint with different shaped sponges

Toddler's Name: _____Ben (Enter Last Name)_____   Caregiver: _____Ms. Hill_____

Date Initiated: _____6/23_____   Date Completed: _____7/16_____

Figure 7–10 22–24 Months Activities *(Continued)*

SCENTED PLAY DOUGH

The delightful color and smell of this dough make it quite popular with children. This dough is nontoxic but does not taste good. Store unused portions in the refrigerator in a tightly sealed container for up to two weeks, or use individual containers such as margarine containers labeled with each child's name to prevent cross-contamination.

Yield: 8 portions

Ingredients:

2½ cups flour

1 cup salt

2 packages unsweetened flavored drinks such as Kool-Aid

3 teaspoons vegetable oil

2 cups hot water

Directions:

1. In a large mixing bowl, mix together all dry ingredients.
2. Pour hot water and oil over dry ingredients and mix well.

Tips:

■ Remind children that this dough is *not* edible.

■ Prolong the life of the play dough by storing it in an airtight plastic container.

Suggestions and Variations:

■ Use grape-flavored drink mix for purple dough, strawberry for red, and so on.

■ Try using a rolling pin and cookie cutters when playing with this dough.

GELATIN BLOCKS

Prepare wonderful wobbly gelatin blocks using a heavy gelatin such as Knox. This type of gelatin is different from the flavored kind. The children may handle it and it is completely edible.

Ingredients:

4 envelopes Knox gelatin

3 packages flavored gelatin (3 oz.), any flavor

4 cups boiling water

In a large bowl, combine the gelatins. Add the water and stir until dissolved. Pour into a shallow pan and chill until firm. You may cut the gelatin into squares, and children can eat them with their hands. Encourage the children to wiggle the squares. Watch the movements and talk about how the gelatin looks and feels. You may instead cut the gelatin with cookie cutters to create many different shapes.

LARGE ICE CUBES

Make large ice cubes by filling empty ½ gallon to 1 gallon paper milk cartons with water. Freeze solid and tear off the outside carton to retrieve your large ice cube. Float in a water table or kitchen wash basin for cold exploration.

FIGURE 7–11 Scented Play Dough, Gelatin Blocks, and Large Ice Cube Activities

PERSONAL SUPPLY INVENTORY CHECKLIST

TODDLER'S NAME: _Jessica (Enter Last Name)_   **DATE:** _9/12_

SUPPLY	FULL	HALF	NEED MORE
Diapers	X		
Disposable wipes		X	
Waterproof paper for diaper barrier (such as wax paper)	X		
Diaper ointment			X
Pacifier/pacifier safety clip	X		
Disposable trainers	X		
Plastic pants covers			
Underwear			
Shirts	X		
Long pants			X
Short pants	X		
Socks			X
Other:			

FIGURE 7–12 Personal Supply Inventory Checklist

Recommend Resources

Alchin, L. K. Nursery rhymes lyrics and origins. Retrieved October 23, 2004, from http://www.rhymes.org.uk

Allen, E. K., & Marotz, L. R. *Developmental profiles pre-birth through twelve* (4th ed.). Clifton Park, NY: Thomson Delmar Learning.

Broad, L. P., & Butterworth, N. T. (1974). *The playgroup handbook.* New York: St. Martin's Press.

Clark, A. (2003). *The ABC's of quality child care.* Clifton Park, NY: Thomson Delmar Learning.

Feldman, J. (2000). *Rainy day activities.* Beltsville, MD: Gryphon House.

5-minute fairy tales. (1999). Lincolnwood, IL: Publications International.

Frailberg, S. H. (1987). *The magic years.* New York: Fireside. (Original work published 1959).

Harrington, C. (1994). ABC Primetime. *From the beginning: Your child's brain.* Los Angeles: American Production.

Herr, J. (1994). *Working with young children.* Tinley Park, IL: The Goodheart-Willcox Company.

Marhoefer, P. E., & Vadnais, L. A. (1988). *Caring for the developing child.* Clifton Park, NY: Thomson Delmar Learning.

Odeon, K. (1998). *Great books for boys.* New York: Ballantine Books.

Stephens, C. G. (2000). *Coretta Scott King Award books.* Englewood, CO: Libraries Unlimited.

United Art & Education Equipment & Supplies, 1-800-322-3247, http://www.UnitedNow.com

Educational Articles for Families and Staff

To find your specific
State's Licensing, Rules
and Regulations go to:

http://nrc.uchsc.edu

This chapter offers short articles relevant for caring for and developing a better understanding of toddlers. Post these articles on the current event bulletin board, include them in program newsletters, or use them as a basis for parenting and staff education classes. Store copies of these articles and other informative articles you collect in the KIDEX Class Book for future reference. The articles include page 97, Impetigo; page 98, Pinworms; page 99, Ringworm; page 100, Toddler Safety; page 101, Help Prevent Choking; page 102, Is Sharing Possible for Toddlers? and page 103, Biting Is a Toddler Affair.

Other books in the KIDEX series contain information on the following:

KIDEX FOR INFANTS

Sudden Infant Death Syndrome
Colds
Respiratory Synctial Virus (RSV)
Strep Throat
Ear Infections
Diarrhea Illness
Diaper Rash
Convulsions/Seizures
Teething

KIDEX FOR TWOS

Mashed Fingers
Chicken Pox
Scabies
Submersion and Drowning Accidents
Tooth Injuries
Temper Tantrums
Toilet Training
Dental Care for Young Children

KIDEX FOR THREES

Vision Screening
Learning from the Process, Not the Outcome
Conducting a Cooking Class for
    Three-Year-Olds
Whining Is a Form of Communication
Questions About Hearing for Young Children
When Does the Learning Start?
Pink Eye

KIDEX FOR FOURS

Is My Child Ready for Kindergarten?
Healthy "Floor Posture"
Bedwetting
My Child Is Shy
Signs of Child Abuse
Styles of Learning
My Child Stutters!

IMPETIGO

What is it?

Impetigo is an infection of the skin, usually caused by bacteria.

What does it look like?

Impetigo generally appears on the face around the nose and mouth as a pus-filled, blister-like rash that may or may not itch. It occurs most commonly during the warm summer months.

What is the incubation period?

The incubation period varies. Commonly it is 1–14 days, depending on the germ causing the infection.

How long is it contagious?

It is contagious as long as the scabbed-over sores (lesions) contain pus, usually one or two weeks, or for 24 hours after antibiotic treatment is started.

How does it spread?

The bacteria spread with direct contact with the sore, contaminated clothing, or linens. Staff members may pass it from child to child if they do not wash their hands thoroughly and often.

What is a proper plan of action?

Isolate the child from other children to reduce possible cross-contamination.
If possible, cover the child's rash area with gauze or a bandage to prevent spreading.
Notify parents.
Seek medical supervision.
Stress thorough hand washing techniques for staff and children.

Who should be notified?

Notify other parents if the case is confirmed. They can watch for symptoms.

When can a child resume contact with other children?

Children can resume contact with others when existing sores are crusted, with no pus under the crusts, or they have been on an antibiotic for at least 24 hours.

What can be done to stop the spread of impetigo?

Stop the spread of impetigo with frequent hand washing after contact with the rash. Cover the rash area with a light bandage or clothing until all sores are crusted.

Recommended Resources

Reisser, P. C., M. (1997). *Baby & child care.* Carol Stream, IL: Tyndale House.
Kemper, K. J., (1996). *The holistic pediatrician.* New York: HarperCollins.

PINWORMS

What is it?
An infestation with white thread-like worms.

What does it look like?
The child may be irritable and experience restlessness while sleeping or may experience an itchy bottom. Sometimes thread-like worms are visible in the child's stool (bowel movement), but more often they are seen on the skin around the anus. The child's anus may become irritated.

What is the incubation period?
3 to 6 weeks.

How long is it contagious?
As long as worms or eggs are present in the stool.

How does it spread?
Pinworm infestation is highly contagious and spreads through the fecal-oral route, which means that the germs in one person's bowel movement wind up in another person's mouth, usually by way of unwashed hands.

What is a proper plan of action?
Notify the child's parents.
Encourage parents to seek medical supervision for treatment and medication.
Teach the other children to wash their hands carefully after using the toilet and before eating.
Sanitize the toilet seat daily with disinfectant.

Who should be notified?
Parents of the infected child.
Other parents and staff so they can watch for signs and symptoms.

When can a child resume contact with other children?
Usually after the course of treatment and upon a doctor's approval.

Recommended Resources
Reisser, P. C., M. (1997). *Baby & child care.* Carol Stream, IL: Tyndale House.
Kemper, K. J., (1996). *The holistic pediatrician.* New York: HarperCollins.

RINGWORM

What is it?
Ringworm is a contagious disease caused by a fungus.

What does it look like?
Ringworm is usually round. It has a slightly raised outer edge and a pinkish center. It may occur on the scalp or any part of the body. It is usually itchy.

What is the incubation period?
10 to 14 days.

How long is it contagious?
It is contagious until effectively treated by a doctor.

How does it spread?
Ringworm is spread by direct or indirect contact with the infected skin or hair of children or animals.

What is a proper plan of action?
Isolate the child.
Call the child's parents.
Recommend medical supervision.
Practice good hygiene to keep ringworms from spreading to other children.

Who should be notified?
Parents of the infected child.

When can a child resume contact with other children?
After treatment and release by a doctor. Once treatment has begun there is usually no need to exclude the child, although you may need to cover infected areas with a light gauze dressing.

Recommended Resources

Reisser, P. C., M. (1997). *Baby & child care.* Carol Stream, IL: Tyndale House.
Kemper, K. J. (1996). *The holistic pediatrician.* New York: HarperCollins.

TODDLER SAFETY

It is in toddlers' nature to explore everything they come into contact with. That intense curiosity is how they build their little databases of knowledge. Everything is new to them. Their exploring expeditions could include touching, feeling, and tasting every new item.

It is understandable why they are targets for accidents. Not only do they lack experience with how their decisions affect their safety, they do not possess the necessary self-control to resist their natural impulses. Leaving toddlers to their own devices isn't much different from setting bulls loose in a china shop! Because they are perpetually moving about and exploring, they must be kept under watchful adult supervision at all times. They are not capable of recognizing danger signals yet. In essence, the adult will need to make decisions for the child until he or she possesses sufficient knowledge.

Put all cleaning products, medicines, small items, and precious heirlooms out of harm's way. If something is poisonous, consider locking it up. A toddler might drink blue window cleaner not knowing it is much different from a blue popsicle! Make sure all doors can be properly latched. If a toddler is able to open a door, consider installing the latch up high, out of his or her reach.

Post basic instructions for performing first aid in emergencies. Contact your local fire department to learn about community classes designed especially to teach life-saving techniques such as first aid, rescue breathing, and CPR. Post emergency numbers by the telephones in your home before an emergency occurs. Include the number for the local fire department, doctor, dentist, and poison control. If an emergency occurs and you need to call one of these numbers, stay on the phone. Do not hang up until you have been instructed to. Frantic parents have been known to hang up before sharing the address where the emergency is occurring. Make every attempt to keep calm until help arrives.

HELP PREVENT CHOKING

Young toddlers and two-year-old children are especially at risk of choking on food because they have a limited number of teeth. They are not able to thoroughly chew their food and will need their food chopped in small pieces for them to eat without difficulty.

Always watch or sit with children during meals and snacks. Encourage them to eat slowly and chew well before swallowing. Adopt a firm rule never to leave the table until they have swallowed their last bite. Cut the foods into small pieces or thin slices. Cut round foods, like hot dogs, lengthwise into thin strips, or run them through a food processor. Steam carrots and celery until they are soft and manageable, and then cut them into tiny bite-size pieces. Remove seeds and pits from fruit, and cut apples into minuscule pieces. A toddler might be able to bite a piece out of a whole apple with his or her front teeth but does not have a complete set of teeth to finish the job.

Foods that bear watching are hot dogs, hard candy, large pieces of fruit, granola, peanuts, whole grapes, and cherries with pits. Avoid serving toddlers popcorn, potato chips, corn chips, or pretzels. Sticky or tough foods that do not break apart easily and are hard to remove from the airway are chunks of peanut butter, pieces of meat, chewing gum, marshmallows, hard candy, and pieces of dried fruit.

If you need to employ first aid measures, follow these procedures:

Check the scene for safety.

- If the child is not able to cough, cry, or take a breath, or if the child is turning a dusky blue color, then the airway most likely obstructed and the child needs help. It requires air to cough, cry, or take in breath.

- Once you have determined the child is not breathing, call 9-1-1 or your local emergency numbers.

- From toddler age up through age eight, if the child is conscious, give abdominal thrusts until the object comes out.

- If the child is not breathing, give one slow breath about every 3 seconds. If air won't go in, give up to five abdominal thrusts, look for and clear any object from his or her mouth, and resume rescue breathing attempts.

- Continue assisting the child's breathing until he or she resumes on his or her own or until emergency personnel arrive and take over the treatment of the victim.

IS SHARING POSSIBLE FOR TODDLERS?

To understand toddler's capacity to share with their peers, it is imperative to understand where they are in development. Just as we would not consider forcing them to grow an inch taller, we cannot push them to accomplish more than they are capable of before they are ready. During the second year their biggest task is to establish themselves as an independent human being. It is safe to say the period between their first birthday and their third will be very self-centered. What adults might see as "selfish" is in reality a very natural and expected state in their development for them to accomplish the task of "unfolding." Understanding their natural patterns of growth and development will help discern what to ignore as a passing phase and what to pay closer attention to.

At times it seems toddlers are in constant motion. They are very busy learning the rudimentary skills of decision making, self-sufficiency, self-discipline, and asserting their influence on others and on the environment they inhabit. They are charged with these tasks, lacking knowledge of acceptable social skills, possessing minimal vocabulary, and in a body that has yet to master mobility, coupled with a driving internal force to go forth! Because of their limited repertoire of development and intense inner drive to break out of their shell, they are bound to experience moments of confusion and great inner turmoil.

Although their vocabulary continues to grow and they are beginning to combine some words, they still are not capable of clearly expressing many of their needs and desires. Along with impulsive behavior, less refined motor skills, and reduced abilities to communicate, they tend to experience many moments of frustration and exhibit challenging behaviors. It is very normal to expect toddlers to begin to test their limits during this time of development. Defiant behavior and the use of the word "no" will surface, in varying degrees, as they test their new levels of independence. When life becomes too overwhelming, toddlers will experience "mini meltdowns" most adults refer to as temper tantrums.

It is probably a good time to discuss their play habits and their ability to share with their peers. It is fair to say they are operating on a short fuse during most of this period. Their growth and development are demanding so much of their self-focus limits their ability to practice the best social skills. Sharing is not a top priority! If they want something they take it. If someone is in their path they might step on them. Biting and hair pulling often are the quickest way to communicate "me first." It is important to encourage them to begin using methods of self-control and self-discipline, but keep in mind that most of them are not up for the task consistently. In short, don't expect them to understand the concept of sharing. Just as they currently lack the capability to cross a busy street by themselves, at this age they do not yet possess enough maturity to share with others.

For the time being, provide duplicates of favorite toys so sharing is not a primary issue, use redirection through distraction, physically move their bodies from temptation or potential harm, remove the object of concern, and create areas for them to play undisturbed until they are able to practice more restraint. Continue to help them understand their desires and help them build their growing vocabulary skills.

As they approach their third birthday, children will become capable of distinguishing between what is yours and what is mine and begin to exercise some degree of self-control in those matters. In the meantime a boatload of energy, understanding, patience, and occasional rest breaks with other sympathetic adults will help you sail through what could be one of the most challenging times in your toddler's early existence.

Recommended Resources

Ames, L. B. P., Ilg, F. L., & C. C. Haber, (1982). *Your one-year-old.* New York: Dell.
Ames, L. B. P., & Ilg, F. L. (1976). *Your two-year-old.* New York: Dell.

BITING IS A TODDLER AFFAIR

Why do toddlers bite?

Very young children sometimes bite others when they are teething, overwhelmed, frustrated, fascinated by the outcome, tired, hungry, thirsty, seeking attention, or simply imitating another child's actions.

If my toddler bites another child how should I handle the situation?

First attend to the bitten child: Cleanse the bite with soap and water. Soothe the skin with an ice pack or cool compress and if the skin is broken make sure the child's tetanus shot is up to date. Notify the bitten child's parents. Report signs of infection such as oozing, redness, pain, or swelling. Within moments of the bite, in a calm but firm voice say, "Biting hurts," or "Your teeth hurt Alexis. Now she is crying."

Is HIV or AIDS transmitted through a bite?

Contracting a case of HIV/AIDS is highly unlikely. In fact, Kinnell (2002) reports "the Center for Disease Control and Prevention stated 'we have never documented a case of HIV being transmitted through biting.' "

Should I punish my toddler if she bites?

Although biting seems cruel, toddlers use it is an impulsive reaction rather than a premeditated act. Avoid overreacting to this in a heated manner and resorting to yelling, slapping, spanking, putting pepper on the biter's tongue or biting the child back. The best approach is to catch children in the act and remove them, make sure they are rested and fed, provide interesting things to do, and help them avoid overwhelming situations, especially involving other young children, until they develop more sophisticated coping skills. In a play group, provide duplicates of favorite toys or remove the item causing the friction.

How come my child's teacher will not tell me the name of the child who bit?

Professional early childhood programs have made a commitment to protect all the children they care for, including maintaining client confidentiality. To avoid labeling any child or to avoid a parent's being approached in an inappropriate manner by a well-meaning or angry parent, confidentiality is the best choice for everyone concerned. Energy is better spent determining the potential causes currently provoking the biting and devising measures to end the behavior.

How should biting be handled in a group of children?

There are always prevailing circumstances that cause a toddler to bite. Isolating the circumstances that are provoking the attacks will help with formulating a plan to circumvent the cause and action. *No Biting*, written by Gretchen Kinnell for the Child Care Council of Onondaga County, is an excellent resource for programs to learn very specific actions to reduce and stop the act of biting when it surfaces in a program.

Reference

Kinnell, G. (2002). *No biting.* St. Paul, MN: Redleaf Press.

References

Ames, L. B. P., Ilg, F. L., & Haber, C. C. (1982). *Your one-year-old. New York: Dell.*

Ames L. B. P., Ilg, F. L. (1976). *Your two-year-old. New York: Dell.*

Kinnell, G. (2002). *No biting. St. Paul, MN: Redleaf Press.*

Kemper, K. J., M., M.P.H. (1996). *The holistic pediatrician. New York: HarperCollins.*

Reisser, P. C., M. (1997). *Baby & child care. Carol Stream, IL: Tyndale House.*

Index

To find your specific
State's Licensing, Rules
and Regulations go to:

http://nrc.uchsc.edu

APPENDIX

A

Forms and Templates

Organized by chapter, this appendix contains the following forms and templates for your convenience.

Cleaning Schedule

For the Week of _____

Classroom _____

Daily Cleaning Projects	Mon	Tue	Wed	Thr	Fri	Once-A-Week Projects	Initial	Date
1. Mop floors						Scrub brush & mop (corners)		
2. Clean all sinks (use cleanser)						Wipe down all bathroom walls		
3. Wipe down walls (around sinks)						Scrub step stools		
4. Clean & disinfect toilets (with brush in & out)						Use toothbrush on fountain (mouth piece)		
5. Clean water fountains/wipe with disinfectant						Clean windows		
6. Clean inside of windows and seals						Wipe off door handles		
7. Clean inside & outside glass on doors						Organize shelves		
8. Clean & disinfect changing table & under the pad						Move furniture and sweep		
9. Run vacuum (carpet & rugs)						Wipe underneath tables & legs		
10. Dispose of trash (replace bag in receptacle)						Wipe chair backs and legs		
11. Wipe outside of all cans & lids with disinfectant						Wipe off cubbies/shelves		
12. Repeat 10 & 11 for diaper pails						(preschool & older groups) Wipe/sanitize toys		
13. Clean & disinfect high chairs/tables/chairs						**Immediate Project**		
14. Clean & disinfect baby beds/cots						Any surface area contaminated with body fluids such as blood, stool, mucus, vomit or urine		
15. Reduce clutter! (Organize!)						**Quarterly**		
16. (infant & toddler groups) Wipe/sanitize toys after each individual use						Clean carpets		
17. Change crib sheets as directed								
18.								

C – Complete   N/A – Not Applicable

Lead Teacher: _____

KIDEX *for* ONES

Class Book

_____
GROUP NAME

DAILY TODDLER SCHEDULE OUTLINE

Early Morning	
Mid Morning	
Late Morning	
Mid Day	
Early Afternoon	
Mid Afternoon	
Late Afternoon	
Early Evening	

DAILY TODDLER SCHEDULE DETAILS

Early Morning	
Mid Morning	
Late Morning	
Mid Day	
Early Afternoon	
Mid Afternoon	
Late Afternoon	
Early Evening	

Introduce Us to Your Toddler
(12 – 36 Months)

Date _____

Last Name: _____ First Name: _____ Middle: _____

Name your child is called at Home: _____

Siblings' Names & Ages: _____

Favorite Play Materials: _____

Special Interests: _____

Pets: _____

What opportunities does your child have to play with others the same age? _____

_____

Eating Patterns:

    Are there any dietary concerns? _____

    Does your child feed himself or herself?_____

    Are there any food dislikes? _____

    Are there any food allergies? _____

    When eating, uses fingers ____ spoon ____ fork ____ needs assistance _____

Sleeping Patterns:

    What time is bedtime at home? _____ Arise at? _____

    What time is nap time? _____ How long? _____

    Does your child have a special toy/blanket to nap with? _____

    How is your child prepared for rest (e.g., story time, quiet play, snack)

    _____

Eliminating Patterns:

    Not potty trained yet? _____ (skip to health patterns)

    In training? _____ If trained, how long? _____

    Independent–doesn't require help. _____

    Does your child need to be reminded? _____

    If yes, at what time intervals? _____

    Does your child have certain words to indicate a need to eliminate? _____

    _____

Child wears:

    Nap time diaper _____ Disposable training pants _____

    Cloth underwear _____ Plastic pants over cloth underwear _____

Stress/Coping Patterns:

    Uses pacifier _____ Brand _____

    Does your child have any fears: _____ Storms _____ Separation anxiety ____

        Dark _____ Animals _____ Stranger anxiety _____

        Being alone _____ Other _____

    How do you soothe him or her? _____

Health Patterns:

    List any medications, intervals, and route (mouth, ears, eyes, etc.):

    _____

    List any health issues or special needs: _____

    _____

Activity Patterns:

    When did your child begin: Creeping _____ Crawling _____ Walking _____

Indicate your child's symptoms when teething. _____

_____

Is there any other information we should know in order to help us know your child better?

_____

_____

_____

Other Comments: _____

_____

_____

                              _____

                              Parent/Guardian completing form

---

OFFICE USE ONLY

Start Date: _____ Full Time: _____ Part Time: S M T W T F S ½ a.m. p.m.

Group Assigned: a.m. _____ p.m. _____

Caregiver(s): _____

Please keep an adjustment record for _____ weeks.

Assign a cubby space: _____ Assign a diaper space: _____

KIDEX for Toddlers
Individual Monthly Profile

Month: _____ Caregivers: _____

Child's Name: _____ Group: _____

Age: _____ Birth Date: _____ Allergies: _____

Parents'/Guardians' Names: _____ Start Date:_____

Special Blanket/Toy: _____ Pacifier Type:_____

Diapers: _____ Nap time Diaper Only:_____ *Potty Trained:_____

Independent: _____ Needs reminding: _____ Potty training: _____

Special Diapering Instructions (special ointments, etc): _____

Personality Traits: shy/reserved   outgoing/curious   sensitive/frightens easily
(Circle all that apply)   very verbal   active   restless
                            cuddly   demonstrative   stranger anxiety
                            cautious

Dietary Patterns: needs help _____ uses spoon/fork independently _____

Food Dislikes: _____

Health Concerns: _____

Daily Medications: yes _____   no _____   (see med sheet for details)

Special Needs Instructions: _____

Stress/Coping Pattern: fears _____   storms _____   loudness _____   strangers _____
          dark _____   animals _____   separation anxiety _____   others _____

Number of Naps: 1 or 2   Average Nap Length: AM _____to_____   PM _____to_____

Special Nap Instructions: _____

_____

Favorite Activities This Month: _____

Days Attending: Sun.   Mon.   Tues.   Wed.   Thurs.   Fri.   Sat.   1/2 days Full days

Approximate Arrival Time _____   Approximate Departure Time _____

Those authorized to pick up: _____

Warning: If name is not listed, consult with office and obtain permission to release child. If you are not familiar with this person, always request I.D.

* The majority of toddlers potty train at ages 2½ –3 years

PROGRAM ENROLLING APPLICATION

Child's Full Name: _____ Nickname: _____

Date of Birth: _____ Sex: _____ Home Phone: _____

Address: _____ City: _____ Zip Code: _____

Legal Guardian: _____

Mother's Name: _____ Home Phone: _____

Cell Phone: _____ E-mail: _____

Address: _____ City: _____ Zip Code: _____

Employer: _____ Work Phone: _____

Address: _____ City: _____ Zip Code: _____

Father's Name: _____ Home Phone: _____

Cell Phone: _____ E-mail: _____

Address: _____ City: _____ Zip Code: _____

Employer: _____ Work Phone: _____

Address: _____ City: _____ Zip Code: _____

IN THE EVENT YOU CANNOT BE REACHED IN AN EMERGENCY, CALL:

Name: _____ Relationship: _____ Phone: _____

Address: _____ City: _____ Zip Code: _____

Name: _____ Relationship: _____ Phone: _____

Address: _____ City: _____ Zip Code: _____

OTHER PEOPLE RESIDING WITH CHILD

Name: _____ Relationship: _____ Age: _____

Name: _____ Relationship: _____ Age: _____

Name: _____ Relationship: _____ Age: _____

PEOPLE AUTHORIZED TO REMOVE CHILD FROM THE CENTER

Your child will not be allowed to go with anyone unless their name appears on this application, or you provide them with an "authorization card," or you make other arrangements with the management. Positive I.D. will be required.

Name: _____ Relationship: _____

Name: _____ Relationship: _____

Name: _____ Relationship: _____

Child Will Attend: Mon - Tues - Wed - Thur - Fri - Sat - Sun

Child Will Be: Full Time or Part Time

Time Child Will Be Dropped Off (Normally): _____

Time Child Will Be Picked Up (Normally): _____

MEDICAL INFORMATION/AUTHORIZATION

Physician's Name: _____ Phone: _____

Address: _____ City: _____ Zip Code: _____

Dentist's Name: _____ Phone: _____

Address: _____ City: _____ Zip Code: _____

Allergies: _____

I agree and give consent that, in case of accident, injury, or illness of a serious nature, my child will be given medical attention/emergency care. I understand I will be contacted immediately, or as soon as possible if I am away from the numbers listed on this form.

PERMISSION TO LEAVE PREMISES

I hereby give the school/center _____ permission to take my child

on neighborhood walks using a _____ (state equipment, e.g., a

child buggy that seats six children & has safety straps). YES_____(INITIAL)

NO, I do not give permission at this time: _____ (INITIAL)

Parent/Guardian's Signature: _____

Parent/Guardian's Signature: _____

Date: _____

AUTHORIZED
PERSON
CARD

AUTHORIZED
PERSON
CARD

AUTHORIZED
PERSON
CARD

AUTHORIZED
PERSON
CARD

AUTHORIZED
PERSON
CARD

AUTHORIZED
PERSON
CARD

AUTHORIZED
PERSON
CARD

AUTHORIZED
PERSON
CARD

AUTHORIZED
PERSON
CARD

AUTHORIZED
PERSON
CARD

USE HEAVY CARD STOCK (FRONT OF CARD)

Name of Authorized Person

May pick up my child _____

on my behalf.

_____ _____
Parent/Guardian Signature   Date

Name of Authorized Person

May pick up my child _____

on my behalf.

_____ _____
Parent/Guardian Signature   Date

Name of Authorized Person

May pick up my child _____

on my behalf.

_____ _____
Parent/Guardian Signature   Date

Name of Authorized Person

May pick up my child _____

on my behalf.

_____ _____
Parent/Guardian Signature   Date

Name of Authorized Person

May pick up my child _____

on my behalf.

_____ _____
Parent/Guardian Signature   Date

Name of Authorized Person

May pick up my child _____

on my behalf.

_____ _____
Parent/Guardian Signature   Date

Name of Authorized Person

May pick up my child _____

on my behalf.

_____ _____
Parent/Guardian Signature   Date

Name of Authorized Person

May pick up my child _____

on my behalf.

_____ _____
Parent/Guardian Signature   Date

Name of Authorized Person

May pick up my child _____

on my behalf.

_____ _____
Parent/Guardian Signature   Date

Name of Authorized Person

May pick up my child _____

on my behalf.

_____ _____
Parent/Guardian Signature   Date

USE HEAVY CARD STOCK (BACK OF CARD)

Toddler Daily Observation Checklist

Child's name: _____   Date: _____

Arrival: _____   Departure: _____

	Ate Partial	Ate Complete	Oz. Formula
Breakfast			
Snack			
Lunch			
Snack			
Mini Snack			
Dinner			
Evening Snack			

	Medications *	Treatments *
Time		
Time		
Time		

* see daily medication sheets for details

Diaper Changes				
Time	**Wet**	**BM**	**Dry**	**Initials**
9:00 a				
11:00 a				
1:45 p				
4:15 p				

Nap Times: _____   _____   Other: _____

Potty Training Progress					
Time	**Wet**	**Dry**	**Bowel Movement**	**Accident Clothing Change**	**Seemed confused upset/resisted/refused re-evaluate readiness**

Moods / Activity Level:
Circle all that apply
Busy • Curious • Adventurous • Active • Cheerful • Quiet • Content • Cuddly • Drowsy • Bubbly • Verbal • Defiant • Focused • Frustrated Easily

Today's Play Center Choices: _____   _____

Comments: _____

_____

_____

_____

_____

Lead Caregiver: _____
Shift Time: _____
Caregiver: _____
Shift Time: _____
Caregiver: _____
Shift Time: _____
Caregiver: _____
Shift Time: _____
Caregiver: _____
Shift Time: _____

Diaper Changing Procedures for Disposable Diapers

Supplies: Disposable nonabsorbent gloves, nonabsorbent paper liner disposable wipes removed from container, child's personally labeled ointments (under medical direction) diapers, cotton balls, plastic bags, tissues, physician-prescribed lotions, lidded hands-free plastic-lined trash container, soap, disinfectant, and paper towels.

Use a nonabsorbent changing surface. Avoid dangerous falls: keep a hand on baby at all times and never leave alone. In emergency, put child on floor or take with you.

	Steps for Changing Disposable Diapers				
1	Wash hands with soap and water.	2	Gather supplies.	3	Put on disposable waterproof gloves (if used).
4	Cover diapering surface with nonabsorbent paper liner.	5	Place baby on prepared diapering area (minimize contact: hold baby away from your body if extremely wet or soiled).	6	Put soiled clothes in a plastic bag.
7	Unfasten diaper. Leave soiled diaper under the child.	8	Gently wash baby's bottom. Remove stool and urine from front to back, and use a fresh wipe each time. Dispose directly in designated receptacle.	9	Fold soiled diaper inward and place in designated receptacle followed by the disposable gloves (if used).
10	Use disposable wipe to clean surface of caregiver's hands and another to clean the child's.	11	Check for spills on paper. If present, fold over so fresh part is under buttocks.	12	Place clean diaper under baby.
13	Using a cotton ball or tissue, apply skin ointment to clean, dry area if indicated/ordered.	14	Fasten diaper and dress with fresh clothing.	15	Wash baby's hands with soap and water between 60°F and 120°F for 15–20 sec. and dry. Turn faucet off with a paper towel, then place baby in a safe location.
16	Clean and disinfect diapering area, leaving bleach solution in contact at least 2 minutes. Allow table to air dry, or wipe it after 2 minutes.	17	Wash your hands with soap and water for at least 15–20 seconds. Turn off faucet with paper towel.	18	Chart diaper change and any observations.

Standard 3.014 Diaper changing procedure. *Caring for our children, National health and safety performance standards* (2nd ed.).
Used with permission, American Academy of Pediatrics. Permission to photocopy is granted by Thomson Delmar Learning.

Diaper Changing Procedures for Cloth Diapers

Supplies: Disposable nonabsorbent gloves, non absorbent paper liner, disposable wipes removed from container, child's personally labeled ointments (under medical direction), diapers, cotton balls, plastic bags, tissues, physician-prescribed lotions, lidded hands-free plastic-lined trash container, soap, disinfectant, and paper towels.

Soiled Diapers: *Contain in a labeled and washable plastic-lined receptacle that is tightly lidded and hands-free only. Don't require separate bags. However, any soiled diapers sent home are to be secured in a plastic bag, separately bagged from soiled clothing. Clean and disinfect receptacle daily and dispose of waste water in toilet or floor drain only.*

Use a nonabsorbent changing surface. Avoid dangerous falls: keep a hand on baby at all times and never leave alone. In emergency, put child on floor or take with you.

	Steps for Changing Cloth Diapers				
1	Wash hands with liquid soap and water.	2	Gather supplies.	3	Put on disposable waterproof gloves (if used).
4	Cover diapering surface with nonabsorbent paper liner.	5	Place baby on prepared diapering area (minimize contact: hold baby away from your body if extremely wet or soiled).	6	Put soiled clothes in a plastic bag.
7	Unfasten diaper. Leave soiled diaper under the child. Close each safety pin immediately out of child's reach. Never hold pins in mouth.	8	Gently wash baby's bottom. Remove stool and urine from front to back, and use a fresh wipe each time. Dispose directly in designated receptacle.	9	Fold soiled diaper inward and place in designated receptacle followed by the disposable gloves (if used).
10	Use disposable wipe to clean surface of caregiver's hands and another to clean the child's.	11	Check for spills on paper. If present, fold over so fresh part is under buttocks.	12	Place clean diaper under baby.
13	Using a cotton ball or tissue, apply skin ointment to clean, dry area if indicated/ordered.	14	Fasten diaper with pins, placing your hand between the child and the diaper on insertion, and dress with fresh clothing.	15	Wash baby's hands with soap and water between 60°F and 120°F for 15–20 sec. and dry. Turn faucet off with a paper towel, then place baby in a safe location.
16	Clean and disinfect diapering area, leaving bleach solution in contact at least 2 minutes. Allow table to air dry, or wipe it after 2 minutes.	17	Wash your hands with soap and water for at least 15–20 seconds. Turn off faucet with paper towel.	18	Chart diaper change and any observations.

Standard 3.014 Diaper changing procedure. *Caring for our children, National health and safety performance standards* (2nd ed.). Used with permission, American Academy of Pediatrics. Permission to photocopy is granted by Thomson Delmar Learning.

Return Practice Demonstration for Disposable Diapering Procedures

Name: _____   Date: _____

Observer: _____

Procedure:

_____   Wash hands with liquid soap and water.

_____   Gather supplies.

_____   Put on disposable waterproof gloves (if used).

_____   Cover diapering surface with nonabsorbent paper liner.

_____   Place baby on prepared diapering area (minimize contact: hold baby away from your body if extremely wet or soiled).

_____   Put soiled clothes in a plastic bag.

_____   Unfasten diaper. Leave soiled diaper under the child.

_____   Gently wash baby's bottom. Remove stool and urine from front to back, and use a fresh wipe each time. Dispose directly in designated receptacle.

_____   Fold soiled diaper inward and place in designated receptacle followed by the disposable gloves (if used).

_____   Use disposable wipe to clean surface of caregiver's hands and another to clean the child's.

_____   Check for spills on paper. If present, fold over so fresh part is under buttocks.

_____   Place clean diaper under baby.

_____   Using a cotton ball or tissue, apply skin ointment to clean, dry area if indicated/ordered.

_____   Fasten diaper and dress with fresh clothing.

_____   Wash baby's hands with soap and water between 60°F and 120°F for 15–20 seconds and dry. Turn faucet off with a paper towel, then place baby in a safe location.

_____   Clean and disinfect diapering area, leaving bleach solution in contact at least 2 minutes. Allow table to air dry, or wipe it after 2 minutes.

_____   Wash your hands with soap and water for at least 15–20 seconds. Turn off faucet with paper towel.

_____   Chart diaper change and any observations.

Return Practice Demonstration for Cloth Diapering Procedures

Name: _____   Date: _____

Observer: _____

Procedure:

_____   Wash hands with liquid soap and water.

_____   Gather supplies.

_____   Put on disposable waterproof gloves (if used).

_____   Cover diapering surface with nonabsorbent paper liner.

_____   Place baby on prepared diapering area (minimize contact: hold baby away from your body if extremely wet or soiled).

_____   Put soiled clothes in a plastic bag.

_____   Unfasten diaper. Leave soiled diaper under the child. Close each safety pin immediately out of child's reach. Never hold pins in mouth.

_____   Gently wash baby's bottom. Remove stool and urine from front to back, and use a fresh wipe each time. Dispose directly in designated receptacle.

_____   Fold soiled diaper inward and place in designated receptacle followed by the disposable gloves (if used).

_____   Use disposable wipe to clean surface of caregiver's hands and another to clean the child's.

_____   Check for spills on paper. If present, fold over so fresh part is under buttocks.

_____   Place clean diaper under baby.

_____   Using a cotton ball or tissue, apply skin ointment to clean, dry area if indicated/ordered.

_____   Fasten diaper with pins, placing your hand between the child and the diaper on insertion, and dress with fresh clothing.

_____   Wash baby's hands with soap and water between 60°F and 120°F for 15–20 seconds and dry. Turn faucet off with a paper towel, then place baby in a safe location.

_____   Clean and disinfect diapering area, leaving bleach solution in contact at least 2 minutes. Allow table to air dry, or wipe it after 2 minutes.

_____   Wash your hands with soap and water for at least 15–20 seconds. Turn off faucet with paper towel.

_____   Chart diaper change and any observations.

POTTY TRAINING

Child's Name:_____
Primary Caregiver:_____ Date:_____

Time	Wet	B.M.	Dry	Refused	Seemed Confused	Comments
6:00 – 6:30						
6:30 – 7:00						
7:00 – 7:30						
7:30 – 8:00						
8:00 – 8:30						
8:30 – 9:00						
9:00 – 9:30						
9:30 – 10:00						
10:00 – 10:30						
10:30 – 11:00						
11:00 – 11:30						
11:30 – 12:00						
12:00 – 12:30						
12:30 – 1:00						
1:00 – 1:30						
1:30 – 2:00						
2:00 – 2:30						
2:30 – 3:00						
3:00 – 3:30						
3:30 – 4:00						
4:00 – 4:30						
4:30 – 5:00						
5:00 – 5:30						
5:30 – 6:00						
6:00 – 6:30						
6:30 – 7:00						
7:00 – 7:30						
7:30 – 8:00						

Posted Hand Washing Procedures

1	Turn on warm water and adjust to comfortable temperature.	2	Wet hands and apply soap.	3	Wash vigorously for approximately 15ñ20 seconds.
4	Dry hands with paper towel.	5	Turn off faucet with paper towel.	6	Dispose of paper towel in a lidded trash receptacle with a plastic liner.

Use hand washing procedures for staff and children

- before and after preparing bottles or serving food.
- before and after diapering or toileting.
- before and after administering first aid.
- before and after giving medication.
- before working with the children and at the end of the day.
- before leaving the classroom for a break.
- after wiping nose discharge, coughing, or sneezing.
- before and after playing in the sand and water table.
- after playing with pets.
- after playing outdoors.

Daily Medication Sheet

Chilld's Name	RX Number & Type of Medication	Amount & Route Administered	Date	Time	Given By:	
					First Name	Last Name

Medical Authorization
For Nonprescription Medication*

Name of Child: _____   Date: _____

The staff is authorized to dispense the following medications as ordered by your physician and directed by the parents/guardian.

Please indicate specific medication, route it is to be given, dosage, and frequency.

Type	Medication	Route	Dosage	Frequency
Nonaspirin Preparation				
Aspirin Preparation				
Cough Preparation				
Decongestant				
Skin Ointment				
Diaper Wipes				
Sunscreen				

_____   _____   _____
Print Name of Physician   Signature of Physician   Phone Number

_____
Parent/Guardian Signature

Complete this form on admission and update annually. Store medical authorizations in an index box and place in or near locked cabinet for quick referencing.

SUGGESTED ILLNESS

Child's name: _____   Date: _____

SYMPTOMS ARE:

_____   Body Temperature (under arm, add 1 degree)

_____   Vomiting

_____   Diarrhea

_____   Exhibiting signs of a communicable illness

_____   Skin condition requiring further treatment

Other: _____

Report initiated by: _____

Were parents notified? Yes _____ No _____ By whom? _____

Time parents notified: 1st Attempt _____   _____
                                                      Which Parent Notified

                           2nd Attempt _____   _____
                                                      Which Parent Notified

                           3rd Attempt _____   _____
                                                      Which Parent Notified

Time child departed: _____

Director's signature: _____

Children exhibiting a temperature that exceeds 100°F, symptoms of vomiting (1–3 forceful rushes), diarrhea (defined as watery, mucous, foul-smelling bowel movement), or an unrecognized rash shall not return to group care for a minimum of 24 hours after treatment or before symptoms subside.

1. Office Copy   2. Parent/Guardian Copy

Illness Tracking Reports

Name of Child	Date	Time Called	Type of Illness	Person Reporting Illness	Director Notified	Report Filed	Parent Notified	Time Left

Head Lice Checklist

Group Name: _____

Name	Sunday	Monday	Tuesday	Wednesday	Thursday	Friday	Saturday

C = Clear   **A = Absent**   **P = Possible**

(**Reminder**: *Please check weekly on different days of the week.*)

SUGGESTED FIRST AID DIRECTIVES

CHOKING

(Conscious) - Stand or kneel behind child with your arms around his waist and make a fist. Place thumb side of fist in the middle of abdomen just above the navel. With moderate pressure, use your other hand to press fist into child's abdomen with a quick, upward thrust. Keep your elbows out and away from child. Repeat thrusts until obstruction is cleared or child begins to cough or becomes unconscious.

(Unconscious) - Position child on his back. Just above navel, place heel of one hand on the midline of abdomen with the other hand placed on top of the first. Using moderate pressure, press into abdomen with a quick, upward thrust. Open airway by tilting head back and lifting chin. **If you can see the object**, do a finger sweep. Slide finger down inside of cheek to base of tongue, sweep object out but be careful not to push the object deeper into the throat. Repeat above until obstruction is removed or child begins coughing. If child does not resume breathing, proceed with artificial respiration (see below).

Infants - Support infant's head and neck. Turn infant face down on your forearm. Lower your forearm onto your thigh. Give four (4) back blows forcefully between infant's shoulder blades with heel of hand. Turn infant onto back. Place middle and index fingers on breastbone between nipple line and end of breastbone. Quickly compress breastbone one-half to one inch with each thrust. Repeat backblows and chest thrusts until object is coughed up, infant starts to cry, cough, and breathe, or medical personnel arrives and takes over.

POISONING

Call Poison Control Center (1-800-382-9097) immediately! Have the poison container handy for reference when talking to the center. Do not induce vomiting unless instructed to do so by a health professional. Check the child's airway, breathing, and circulation.

HEMORRHAGING

Use a protective barrier between you and the child (gloves). Then, with a clean pad, apply firm continuous pressure to the bleeding site for five minutes. Do not move/change pads, but you may place additional pads on top of the original one. If bleeding persists, call the doctor or ambulance Open wounds may require a tetanus shot.

SEIZURE

Clear the area around the child of hard or sharp objects. Loosen tight clothing around the neck. Do not restrain the child. Do not force fingers or objects into the child's mouth. After the seizure is over and if the child is not experiencing breathing difficulties, lay him/her on his/her side until he/she regains consciousness or until he/she can be seen by emergency medical personnel. After the seizure, allow the child to rest. Notify parents immediately. If child is experiencing breathing difficulty, or if seizure is lasting longer than 15 minutes, call an ambulance at once.

ARTIFICIAL RESPIRATION *(Rescue Breathing)*

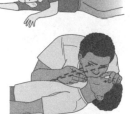

Position child on the back; if not breathing, open airway by gently tilting the head back and lifting chin. Look, listen, and feel for breathing. If still not breathing, keep head tilted back and pinch nose shut. Give two full breaths and then one regular breath every 4 seconds thereafter. Continue for one minute; then look, listen, and feel for the return of breathing. Continue rescue breathing until medical help arrives or breathing resumes.

If using one-way pulmonary resuscitation device, be sure your mouth and child's mouth are sealed around the device.

| (Modification for infants only) | Proceed as above, but place your mouth over nose and mouth of the infant. Give light puffs every 3 seconds. |

SHOCK

If skin is cold and clammy, as well as face pale or child has nausea or vomiting, or shallow breathing, call for emergency help. Keep the child lying down. Elevate the feet. If there are head/chest injuries, raise the head and shoulders only.

To find your specific State's Licensing, Rules and Regulations go to:

http://nrc.uchsc.edu

Accident/Incident

Child's Name: _____

Date of accident/injury: _____ Time: _____

Brief description of accident/injury: _____

_____

_____

Was first aid given? _____ If so, describe: _____

_____

Was blood present in accident? _____ How much? _____

Were Universal Precautions employed? _____

Was medical intervention required?* _____ If yes, describe: _____

_____

Person initiating this report: _____ Witness: _____

Name of parent contacted: _____ Time contacted: _____

Director's signature: _____

*In some states it is required to file a copy of this report with the child care licensing department if medical intervention is required.

Accident/Incident Tracking Reports

Name of Child	Date	Time Called	Type of Accident	Person Reporting Accident	Director Notified	Report Filed	Parent Notified	Time Left

Emergency Contacts: *Post Near Every Telephone*

Your Facility Address: _____

_____

Nearest Main Intersection: _____

Your Facility Phone Number: _____

Contact	Phone Number
Operator	
Emergency	
Fire	
Police	
Consulting Dentist	
Poison Control	
Local Hospital Emergency Dept	
Other	
Other	

Emergency Evacuation Plan (Template)

Draw First Choice Escape Route, Draw Second Choice Escape Route

In Case of Fire Call: _____

In Case of Bomb Threat Call: _____

In Case of Gas Leak Call: _____

Fire Extinguisher expires Date: _____

Emergency Bag and Blanket are located: _____

Place toddlers in the emergency evacuation beds. If the door is cool, open door slowly, make sure fire or smoke isn't blocking your escape route. If your escape is blocked close the door and use alternative escape route. Smoke and heat rise; be prepared to crawl where the air is clearer and cooler near the floor. Move as far from the building as possible. In case of real fire do not reenter the building until it is cleared by the proper authorities.

Hurricane Emergency Instructions

Hurricane/Tropical Storm Watch: indicates the conditions are expected in the specific are usually within 24 hours.

Hurricane/Tropical Storm Warning: conditions are expected within 24 hours.

Send the children home
Learn your specific evacuation route
Secure your facility
Close storm shutters
Turn utilities off at main valves if instructed by authorities
Take emergency phone numbers with you

Your Evacuation Route: _____

_____

_____

Tornado Emergency Instructions

Your county or region is: _____

Tornado Watch: A tornado is possible. Remain alert for approaching storms. Tune your portable (battery-operated) radio to a local weather station.

Tornado Warning: A tornado has been sighted. Activate your emergency shelter plan immediately.

Grab your emergency bag and blanket. They are located: _____

_____

Place the infants in the designated emergency evacuation cribs and move calmly and quickly to an interior room or hallway. Account for all children in attendance.
Your best location is: _____

_____

Cover cribs with a blanket in case of flying glass or debris.

* Avoid windows, doors, outside walls, and corners of rooms.

Earthquake Emergency Instructions

Prior to earthquakes:
- Brace high and top-heavy objects.
- Fasten cubbies, lockers, toy shelves to the wall.
- Anchor overhead lighting fixtures.
- Install flexible pipe fitting to avoid gas or water leaks.
- Know when and how to shut off electricity, gas, and water at main switches and valves.
- Locate safe spots in the room to protect yourself from dropping debris such as under a sturdy table or crib.

Your safest location is: _____

The shutoff for gas is located: _____

The water main is located: _____

Your emergency bag is located: _____

During an earthquake:

- Stay inside until shaking stops and it is safe to go outside.
- Move the infants to your safe location (inside a crib on an inside wall).
- Place a heavy blanket or lightweight mattress over the crib.
- If you are on the playground, move away from the building.

When the shaking stops be prepared for aftershocks. Check for injuries and administer first aid as indicated. Use flashlights if electricity is out. *Do not* light candles or matches in case of gas leakage.

Tornado/Earthquake Drill Log

Date	Time of Drill	Time Needed to Seek Cover	Comments	Full Name of Person in Charge

Building Evacuation Log

Date	Time of Drill	Evacuation Time	Comments	Full Name of Person in Charge

Beginning Our Day   Date: _____

Welcome

Child's Name	Time Awoke	Last Meal/Snack	Last Diaper Change or Toilet Break	Comments, if any

Toddler Weekly Lesson Plans

Stage of Play Development:
Egocentric/Parallel

Group Name: _____

Theme: _____

Lead Caregiver: _____

Week of: _____

Activities	Sun	Mon	Tues	Wed	Thurs	Fri	Sat
Concept							
Sharing Time							
Language Skills							
KIDEX *The Music of Sound* Activities							
Songs/Finger plays							
Reading/Stories (Flannel Board/ Vocabulary/ Puppets)							
Fine Motor Manipulation							
Cognitive/Sensory/Pre-Math/ Science							
KIDEX: *Life is Interesting & My World* Activities							
Arts Exploration/ Crafts							
Gross Motor							
KIDEX: *My Body Is Wonderful* Activities							
Indoor/Outdoor Activities							

Daily Play Centers	Housekeeping/Dramatic Play / Toys Center	Active Play / Music Movement / Toys
	Fine Motor/Art/Eating / Water Table	Library/Music/Quiet Play/Block Center/Computer

Self Help Skills/Social Skills 13-24 Months - Integrate and encourage the development of skills during this 12 month span	Put on and remove shoes & socks with help	Help with cleanup	Body/self-awareness
	Wash & dry hands	Practice yes & no	Safety awareness
	Feed self/rudimentary use of fork & spoon	Practice please & thank you	Follow basic instructions
	Potty training practice (18 months & older only)		

13-15 Months

DEVELOPMENTAL MILESTONES

TODDLERS CAN:

_____ PULL UP TO A STANDING POSITION

_____ MOVE FROM PLACE TO PLACE, HOLDING ON FOR BALANCE

_____ EXPLORE, VERY CURIOUS

_____ PUT OBJECTS INTO A CONTAINER

_____ IMITATE ACTIVITIES DEMONSTRATED

_____ USE, 1 or 2 RECOGNIZABLE WORDS

_____ BEGIN TO DRINK FROM A CUP

_____ BEGIN TO RECOGNIZE AND IDENTIFY OWN BODY PARTS

_____ USE SOME GESTURES SUCH AS WAVING

_____ USE WORDS LIKE _MA-MA_ OR _DA-DA_ INTENTIONALLY

_____ BEND OVER AND PICK UP AN OBJECT

_____ BEGIN TO ATTEMPT WALKING

_____ WALK UP STEPS WITH HELP

_____ USES 3 to 6 WORDS

_____ BUILD A TOWER OF 2 CUBES

_____ IMITATE DUMPING OBJECTS

_____ UNDERSTAND A FEW WORDS

_____ WALK UNAIDED

_____ FIT ROUND BLOCK IN A ROUND HOLE

_____ DRINK FROM A CUP UNASSISTED

_____ POINT TO A DESIRED OBJECT

_____ PUSH, PULL, OR CARRY TOYS WHILE WALKING

_____ ENJOY LOOKING AT BOOKS

_____ SCRIBBLE WITH CRAYON

_____ USE A SPOON INTERMITTENTLY

Important Note: children will develop at similar rates but each in a unique pattern. If you find a child is not exhibiting the majority of characteristics listed, there could be many plausible reasons ranging from premature birth to a more reserved and cautious personality. This list is a broad overview and not inclusive of all developmental milestones toddlers will experience.

TODDLER _____ CAREGIVER _____ DATE _____

Y = YES	S = SOMETIMES	N = NOT YET

16-18 Months

DEVELOPMENTAL MILESTONES

TODDLERS CAN:

_____ IMITATE ACTIVITIES AND BEHAVIORS

_____ ROLL A BALL

_____ IMITATE FEEDING A DOLL OR SOFT TOY

_____ TURNS 2 or 3 PAGES AT A TIME

_____ HAND A TOY TO SOMEONE

_____ FIND A BALL THAT ROLLS OUT OF SIGHT

_____ PLAY A SIMPLE MUSICAL INSTRUMENT (SPOON & PAN)

_____ USE SOME WORDS CORRECTLY, SUCH AS *MA-MA, OH-OH, BYE-BYE*

_____ LATCH ONTO AT LEAST ONE COMFORT HABIT OR OBJECT

_____ BUILDS 2–4 CUBE TOWER

_____ ATTEMPT TO KICK A BALL

_____ BEGIN TO COMBINE WORDS

_____ REMOVE AN ARTICLE OF CLOTHING

_____ UNDERSTAND MANY WORDS AND SIMPLE DIRECTIONS

_____ BEGIN TO THROW A BALL OVERHEAD

_____ TRY TO SING SONGS

_____ POINT AT AND NAME FAMILIAR THINGS

_____ MATCH SAME TOYS

_____ USE SPOON AND FORK BUT NOT EXCLUSIVELY

_____ BEGIN TO ASSIST WITH TOY CLEANUP

_____ PUT UP TO SIX LARGE PEGS INTO A PEGBOARD

_____ ATTEMPT TO JUMP WITH BOTH FEET

_____ FEEL FRUSTRATED EASILY WHEN OVERWHELMED

Important Note: children will develop at similar rates but each in a unique pattern. If you find a child is not exhibiting the majority of characteristics listed, there could be many plausible reasons ranging from premature birth to a more reserved and cautious personality. This list is a broad overview and not inclusive of all developmental milestones toddlers will experience.

TODDLER _____ CAREGIVER _____ DATE _____
Y = YES   S = SOMETIMES   N = NOT YET

19-21 Months

DEVELOPMENTAL MILESTONES

TODDLERS CAN:

_____ ZIP AND UNZIP EASY ZIPPERS WITH ASSISTANCE

_____ SHOW MANY EMOTIONS

_____ EXPERIENCE STRANGER ANXIETY OR SHY BEHAVIOR IN NEW CIRCUMSTANCES

_____ ATTEMPT TO CLAP HANDS TO RHYTHMS

_____ CHATTER MANY WORDS OFTEN MISPRONOUNCED

_____ USE A COUPLE DOZEN WORDS REGULARLY

_____ OFTEN USE NONVERBAL LANGUAGE TO COMMUNICATE

_____ UNDERSTAND SIMPLE INSTRUCTIONS

_____ COPY HOUSEWORK

_____ WASH AND DRY HANDS WITH HELP

_____ USE 50-PLUS SINGLE WORDS

_____ BUILD A TOWER OF 4–6 CUBES

_____ ENJOY SONGS, NURSERY RHYMES, & FINGER PLAYS

_____ BEGIN TO COMBINE WORDS

_____ SPILL DRINK FREQUENTLY

_____ ENJOY PLAY DOUGH, PAINT, PAPER, AND CRAYONS

_____ RIDE SMALL RIDING TOYS WITHOUT PEDALS

_____ TURN FAMILIAR PICTURES RIGHT SIDE UP

_____ USE HER OR HIS OWN NAME

_____ BEGIN TO PUT ON ONE ARTICLE OF CLOTHING

_____ KICK A BALL FORWARD

_____ COMBINE WORDS

> _Important Note: children will develop at similar rates but each in a unique pattern. If you find a child is not exhibiting the majority of characteristics listed, there could be many plausible reasons ranging from premature birth to a more reserved and cautious personality. This list is a broad overview and not inclusive of all developmental milestones toddlers will experience._

| TODDLER _____ CAREGIVER _____ DATE _____ |

| Y = YES | S = SOMETIMES | N = NOT YET |

22-24 Months

DEVELOPMENTAL MILESTONES

TODDLERS CAN:

_____ STRING LARGE BEADS

_____ UNWRAP PACKAGES, ONCE STARTED

_____ JUMP UP

_____ WALK UP STEPS

_____ BEGIN LEARNING GENTLE TOUCHING OF FRAGILE OBJECTS

_____ MATCH SOUNDS TO ANIMALS

_____ LISTEN TO SHORT STORIES

_____ RUN FAST

_____ BEGIN TO COMFORT OTHERS

_____ RECOGNIZE SELF IN A PHOTOGRAPH

_____ UES SHORT SENTENCES

_____ BEGIN USING PREPOSITIONS SUCH AS: *BY, IN, TO, OF*

_____ TURN ONE PAGE AT A TIME (REFINED PINCER GRASP)

_____ LOVE SOUND OF VOICE, ENJOY NOISY OUTBURSTS

_____ ENJOY WATER AND SAND PLAY

_____ SING SOME WORDS TO SOME SONGS

_____ BEGIN USING PRONOUNS SUCH AS I AND ME

_____ BUILD A TOWNER OF 6–8 CUBES

_____ CARRY ON A CONVERSATION WITH 2 or 3 SENTENCES

_____ COPY FOUR WORDS YOU SAY

_____ SPEAK AND BE UNDERSTOOD HALF THE TIME

_____ ASSEMBLE A 1–3 PIECE PUZZLE

_____ DISTINGUISH BETWEEN..."YOURS" AND "MINE"

> *Important Note: children will develop at similar rates but each in a unique pattern. If you find a child is not exhibiting the majority of characteristics listed, there could be many plausible reasons ranging from premature birth to a more reserved and cautious personality. This list is a broad overview and not inclusive of all developmental milestones toddlers will experience.*

TODDLER _____ CAREGIVER _____ DATE _____

| Y = YES | S = SOMETIMES | N = NOT YET |

13–15 Months

ALL ACTIVITIES 2–10 MINUTES

Category 1	**THE MUSIC OF SOUND** **(Sound/Language/Verbal Practice)** • Name things in picture books • Point to and name body parts • Sing "This is the way we wash our face... Comb our hair... Brush our teeth..." • Sing and play "Pat-a-Cake" • Play with a musical jack in the box • Sing "Itsy Bitsy Spider" • Have toddler point to the pictures of animals that you name • Sing Jack and Jill • Use contact paper-covered photos to talk about things a toddler sees every day • Play with xylophone • Use picture books at storytime • Play with spoons and metal pans to build rhythm & sound skills • Look at & discuss old magazines or toy catalogues (replace torn ones to avoid choking from ripped paper) • Tape contact paper-covered pictures up for toddler to look at • Listen to lullaby music during quiet time
Category 2	**MY BODY IS WONDERFUL** **(Large/Fine Motor/Self-Exploration Practice)** • Practice walking—hold child's hand, try different surfaces • Provide push toys such as a toy grocery cart and a baby buggy • Drop wooden clothes pins into a container • Practice stacking with stacking rings • Roll child a ball and encourage child to pick it up and return it to you • Provide child with a bucket filled with plastic blocks for dumping & filling • Mount busy box to wall for busy box play time • At snack time, put oyster crackers in a paper cup to practice picking up small objects • Ask where your nose, eyes, ears, etc. are • Practice hugging and say "Oh, what a nice hug!" • Provide pull toys to pull around the room • Play with a big beach ball

Toddler's Name: _____ Caregiver: _____

Date Initiated: _____ Date Completed: _____

Continued 13–15 Months Activities

Category 3	**MY WORLD** **(Exploring/Emotions/Science/Pre-math Practice)** • Provide a noisemaker for shaking • Blow bubbles and have toddler pop them • Go for a walk and point out different sounds, or use the "see & say" method • Tape contact paper to the wall sticky side out & give toddlers object to stick to it • Practice hanging objects up on hooks attached to a hook board • Paste different leaves on paper and cover with contact paper to talk about • Take special walks as each season changes and talk about each new season • Put ice cubes made from a large container in a water table • Bring out a different animal each week to practice its name • Set up bird feeder outside and watch it through the window • Match pictures in plastic containers with real objects such as keys, a spoon, a ball, a fish, etc. • Look out the window and talk about the weather outside • Fill a plastic can with plastic rings to sort & dump • Take a walk and feel the bark on the trees • Listen to a tape of different weather sounds
Category 4	**LIFE IS INTERESTING** **(Tactile/Cognitive/Touching Practice)** • Use one fat crayon to scribble on a big sheet of paper • Color on dark construction paper with nontoxic colored chalk • Introduce nontoxic finger painting with one color • Give 6" piece masking tape–show places to stick • Fill a pan with a small amount of water and provide a sponge to dip & explore • Provide several sets of nesting blocks to practice stacking • Fill a plastic pop bottle with water, oil, & food coloring, glue cap on securely, and explore • Provide colorful fabric swatches to place on contact paper • Use a colored scarf to hide behind and play peekaboo • Fill a container with cold spaghetti and explore • Make a large scribble book • Call mommy, daddy, or grandparents at work on play telephone • Put out hats to try on and look at in the mirror • Match tools to their silhouettes • Cover a table with taped down paper and finger paint with pudding

Toddler's Name: _____ Caregiver: _____

Date Initiated: _____ Date Completed: _____

16-18 Months

ALL ACTIVITIES 2–15 MINUTES

Category **1**	**THE MUSIC OF SOUND** **(Sound/Language/Verbal Practice)** • Look at animal pictures, make appropriate sounds & encourage imitation • Play music with baby rattles while marching to the sound • Fill a 1/2 gallon jug with 3/4 cup dry beans, glue lid on, and shake to make a great noise maker • Practice "what is this?" by pointing & asking • Play nursery song music • Pull toys out of a box and ask toddler what they are • Use felt pieces for story time–have toddler put the pieces on the board • Help toddlers understand their emotions by describing their feelings • Sing "Where Is Thumpkin?" • Practice language at the table by asking, "Where is your bib?", "cup?", "plate?" etc. • Sing nursery songs & keep rhythm with musical sticks • Look at & talk about book of colors • Play with different size bells & chimes • Ask toddler to bring to you items in the room that you request • Play lively music and dance to it
Category **2**	**MY BODY IS WONDERFUL** **(Large/Fine Motor/Self-Exploration Practice)** • March to band music • Act out "Pop goes the weasel" • Hang a beach ball from the ceiling in a cloth bag to use for punching • Provide several large boxes for toddler to play in • Throw wads of paper into a wide basket • Show how to kick with a large, soft ball • Put tennis balls in a hat, put the hat on, and have fun chasing the balls that fall out • Provide boxes to push around the room • Place a 7"–12" wide flat board on the ground to walk on • Practice jumping off of carpet squares • Push plastic curlers through matching egg carton holes • Put out large pegs and pegboards for matching practice • Play with large stacking blocks

Toddler's Name: _____ Caregiver: _____

Date Initiated: _____ Date Completed: _____

Continued 16–18 Months Activities

Category 3	**MY WORLD** **(Exploring/Emotions/Science/Pre-math Practice)** • Blow air through a straw so toddler can feel the "wind" • Make a "noisy" book out of wax paper—glue pictures of various animals • Bring flowers to touch & smell under supervision • Hang up pictures of dogs & cats to look at • Sit on a blanket inside or outside for story time • Look in a mirror and make faces—encourage toddler to copy you • Sit on big blanket outside while eating snack • Put pictures of tropical fish in a magnetic photo book to look at • Play scoop & pour with oatmeal or sand outdoors • Bring in toddler-friendly animals for a short visit • Provide wet sponges to wash toys • Put a blanket & toys in the shade, in the sun, and indoors on rainy days, and talk about each environment • Collect a bug in a plastic jar for toddler to watch • Provide a goldfish to watch • Talk about happy, sad, angry, and frightened • Put chairs in a single file, sit toddler on each chair & take an imaginary bus ride
Category 4	**LIFE IS INTERESTING** **(Tactile/Cognitive/Touching Practice)** • Smell 3 or 4 different fragrances found on cotton balls, inside of plastic salt & pepper shakers • Make milk shakes together for an afternoon snacks • Tape drawing paper over sandpaper for textured scribble • Give each toddler a pan full of 2" blocks to dump & fill • Give each toddler a purse: demo how to fill, dump and carry their treasurers • Tape paper over netting material for textured scribble • Wash dishes with soapy water in a water table • Explore sandpaper, velvet, and satin for rough, soft, and smooth textures • Make a ramp from 3"–4" wide board to run cars down • Set out dolls in dishpans with blankets for each toddler • Set table with dishes & pretend kitchen items • Wash baby dolls with several dishpans of water, (1" deep water only) • Use glue & glitter to decorate pictures (e.g., snowflakes, leaves, fish, flowers) • Play with sorting cubes • Bring in fist-size rocks, smooth & rough, and explore

Toddler's Name: _____   Caregiver: _____

Date Initiated: _____   Date Completed: _____

19-21 Months

ALL ACTIVITIES 5–20 MINUTE

Category **1**	**THE MUSIC OF SOUND** **(Sound/Language/Verbal Practice)** • Play with a variety of musical instruments • Use puppets to practice children's names • Help describe words to toddler that express happy feelings • Sing "Did You Ever See a Lassie" • Darken the room & describe things you see with a flashlight • Help toddler describe frustrating feelings using words • Use puppets to practice different vocabulary words • Copy sounds you hear such as cars and planes and encourage toddler to repeat • Read books about people who work such as doctors, firefighters, police officers, etc. • Hold baby dolls and/or stuffed animals while singing "Rock-a-Bye Baby" • Explore loud & soft sounds with musical instruments • "Open, shut them", finger play • Sing nursery rhymes • Tape-record toddlers' voices and play back • Play a tape with different kinds of transportation sounds
Category **2**	**MY BODY IS WONDERFUL** **(Large/Fine Motor/Self-Exploration Practice)** • Give toddler a soft animal or doll to carry on your walk • Play with zippers • Play with pop beads • Play with large blocks for stacking • Crawl around and pretend to be different animals • Fill a paper cup with shaving cream & have toddler spread it on a tray • Build with large bristle blocks or duplo blocks • Brush or comb a doll's or stuffed animal's hair with a comb or brush • Provide riding toys without pedals • Practice rolling different size balls to toddler • Put a small toy in a large, empty matchbox and show how to open it • Stick a piece of masking tape on toddler's clothing and practice peeling it off

Toddler's Name: _____ Caregiver: _____

Date Initiated: _____ Date Completed: _____

Continued 19–21 Months Activities

Category **3**	**MY WORLD** **(Exploring/Emotions/Science/Pre-Math Practice)** • Blow bubbles in pan of water with straws—put a hole in the straw to avoid sucking • Take a walk & say words for as many things that you see as you can • Hang "wind sock" outside of window & talk about the wind • Hang up pictures of different kinds of transportation • Lie on the floor and make pretend snow angels • Lie on your back and look at the clouds or pictures on the ceiling • Provide a small amount of water & sponges to wash furniture • Take a walk inside and outside to feel the different textures • Look at pictures of different kinds of horses • Play with 2-piece puzzles of animals made from cutting pictures in two • Bring different size feathers to the room to explore • Play with bubble blowing outside • Bring to a petting zoo or explore zoo animals with a book • Read stories about the seasons • Practice laughing—explore pictures of toddlers having fun
Category **4**	**LIFE IS INTERESTING** **(Tactile/Cognitive/Touching Practice)** • Make flavored play dough—use while warm! • Put string (no longer than 12" long) around stuffed animals and use to pull animals around and to pretend walking a pet • Paint with sand & paint on construction paper • Spread peanut butter on crackers for snacks • Glue packing peanuts to a picture and paint to make packing peanut picture • Provide dress-up clothes for pretend dress-up • Put out a pile of large socks and practice them putting on • Finger paint on paper plates • Match colors with mittens, socks, or flowers) • Play store with used food boxes • Use different colored water markers to draw with finger paint a picture of a pig with mud • Play with gelatin blocks • Color a flower and glue a perfumed cotton ball in the middle of it • Taste different flavors: pickles, lemon, ice cream • Sprinkle sand on pictures prepped with glue

Toddler's Name: _____ Caregiver: _____

Date Initiated: _____ Date Completed: _____

22-24 Months

ALL ACTIVITIES 5–20 MINUTES

Category **1**	### THE MUSIC OF SOUND **(Sound/Language/Verbal Practice)** • Sing "Rain Rain Go Away"—use gestures • Practice everyone's name—have each toddler say his or her name • Sing "Old McDonald" and point out animals in a picture book • Read nursery rhymes at story time • Explore object flash cards • Play teddy bear, teddy bear • Practice saying 3 or 4 words at a time and then have toddler repeat • Tape family members on each finger and sing "Where is...?" • Sing "This Is the Way We Wash Our Clothes" • Look at and discuss a Richard Scarry book like *Things That Go* • Sing "The Wheels On the Bus" • Have a puppet point out objects for toddler to name • Play musical instruments • Talk about family members • Roll ball to toddler and say child's full name
Category **2**	### MY BODY IS WONDERFUL **(Large/Fine Motor/Self-Exploration Practice)** • Practice understanding gentle touching of friends & fragile things • Use small, low slide—assist with sliding • Use a sponge to squeeze water out into a bowl & then pick the water back up with a sponge • Cut large straws in thirds—lace with shoe lace • Practice screwing lids on plastic jars • Play follow the leader with cheerful music playing • Take shoes off, sit, and practice touching your toes • Roll small cars through a paper towel tube • Put long pieces of masking tape on the floor and practice stepping over the tape • Practice standing on one foot at a time • String large beads w/ a shoelace (wrap ends with masking tape) • Play with 2–4 piece puzzles

Toddler's Name: _____ Caregiver: _____

Date Initiated: _____ Date Completed: _____

Continued 22–24 Months Activities

Category 3	**MY WORLD** **(Exploring/Emotions/Science/Pre-math Practice)** • Explore different size/shape shells (use a safe size) • Make a large ice cube in a milk carton to explore during water table time • Bring different types of tree leaves in to feel • Play a tape that explores different water sounds • Hang up pictures of different farm animals • Use big tweezers to transfer small objects into different containers • Explore the feel & shape of pine cones • Play a tape that explores different insects like crickets • Dance outdoors or indoors with scarves & animals • Hang up pictures of the sun & the moon • Put oatmeal or cornmeal in the water table to play with • Take walking excursion and provide a pretend camera to photograph with • Use imitation play—toddler start as seed, then the teacher waters the seed, the seed grows into a plant and moves with the wind • Dance outdoors or indoors with scarves & stuffed animals • Explore things that open & shut • Practice "helping" a sad stuffed animal friend
Category 4	**LIFE IS INTERESTING** **(Tactile/Cognitive/Touching Practice)** • Paint with water pictures or use a brush & water on a side wall • Dress stuffed animals with large t-shirts & hats • Make binoculars from toilet paper rolls & decorate • Explore hot & cold—what different textures do we feel? Soft, hard, etc. • Go to a restaurant, take pretend orders and eat pretend food • Make masks out of paper plates, cut holes for eyes, and look in the mirror • Practice dressing dolls • Fingerpaint with different colors on an individual square, then make a class quilt • Decorate sugar cookies to eat for snack • Play follow the leader • Set up play areas and when interested toddlers join in, move on to set up new areas • Practice ripping up old magazines • Use pieces of fruit like a ½ orange or a cucumber to put in paint and stamp onto paper • Trace each hand, color, and add names to each finger to build a name tree • Paint with different shaped sponges

Toddler's Name: _____ Caregiver: _____

Date Initiated: _____ Date Completed: _____

PERSONAL SUPPLY INVENTORY CHECKLIST

TODDLER'S NAME: _____ **DATE:** _____

SUPPLY	FULL	HALF	NEED MORE
Diapers			
Disposable wipes			
Waterproof paper for diaper barrier (such as wax paper)			
Diaper ointment			
Pacifier/pacifier safety clip			
Disposable trainers			
Plastic pants covers			
Underwear			
Shirts			
Long pants			
Short pants			
Socks			
Other:			

To find your specific
State's Licensing, Rules
and Regulations go to:

http://nrc.uchsc.edu

APPENDIX

Gloving

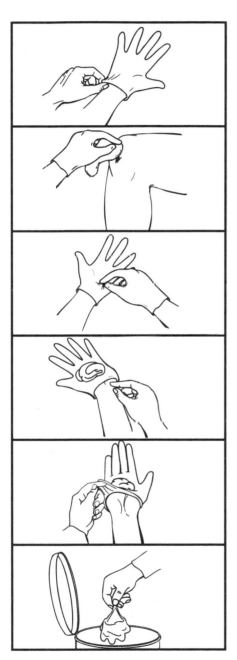

Put on a clean pair of gloves.

Provide the appropriate care.

Remove each glove carefully. Grab the first glove at the palm and strip the glove off. Touch dirty surfaces only to dirty surfaces.

Ball-up the dirty glove in the palm of the other gloved hand.

With the clean hand strip the glove off from underneath at the wrist, turning the glove inside out. Touch dirty surfaces only to dirty surfaces.

Discard the dirty gloves immediately in a step can. Wash your hands.

Reference: California Department of Education. *Keeping Kids Healthy: Preventing and Managing Communicable Disease in Child Care.* Sacramento, CA: California Department of Education, 1995.

Washing Hands

1) Wet hands.

2) Add soap.

3) Rub hands together.

4) Rinse hands with fingers down.

5) Dry your hands with a towel.

6) Turn off water with paper towel.

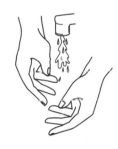

7) Toss the paper towel in the trash.

Good Job!

Reprinted with permission from the National Association of Child Care Professionals, http://www.naccp.org.